Thomas Crosby and the Tsimshian

When the Methodist missionary Thomas Crosby arrived in Port Simpson in northwestern British Columbia in 1874, he did so at the invitation of the Tsimshian people. Earlier contact with the Anglican missionary William Duncan had convinced them that, although many aspects of his mission program were appealing, his brand of religion was too austere. Instead they preferred the more expressive version represented by the Methodist Church.

In *Thomas Crosby and the Tsimshian*, Clarence Bolt demonstrates that the Tsimshian were conscious participants in the acculturation and conversion process – as long as this met their goals – and not merely passive recipients. He argues that in order to understand the complexities of Native-European contacts, one must look at the reasons for Native, as well as for European, behaviour. He points out that Natives actively influenced the manner in which their relationships with the white population developed, often resulting in a complex interaction in which the values of both groups influenced each other.

As long as the conversion process unfolded as they wished, the Tsimshian supported their missionary. Once they realized, however, that the church could not resolve such issues as the land question, they moved away from Crosby.

This book is unique in that it examines the functioning of two missions to the same people in a single locale, demonstrating how a particular Native group tried to protect its traditional land resource while at the same time seeking participation in the emerging White society of nineteenth-century British Columbia.

CLARENCE BOLT is an instructor in the Department of History at Camosun College in Victoria.

CLARENCE BOLT

Thomas Crosby and the Tsimshian
Small Shoes for Feet Too Large

UBC Press / Vancouver

© UBC Press 1992
All rights reserved
Printed in Canada on acid-free paper ∞

ISBN 0-7748-0430-0

Canadian Cataloguing in Publication Data

Bolt, Clarence R.
Thomas Crosby and the Tsimshian

Includes bibliographical references and index.
ISBN 0-7748-430-0

1. Crosby, Thomas, 1840-1914. 2. Tsimshian Indians – Cultural assimilation. 3. Tsimshian Indians – Religion and mythology. 4. Tsimshian Indians – Missions – History. 5. Indians of North America – British Columbia – Port Simpson – Cultural assimilation. 6. Indians of North America – British Columbia – Port Simpson – Religion and mythology. 7. Indians of North America – British Columbia – Port Simpson – Missions – History. 8. Methodist Church – Missions – British Columbia – Port Simpson – History. I Title.

E99.T8B64 1992   306'.089'974 C92-092626-0

This book has been published with the help of a grant from the Social Science Federation of Canada, using funds provided by the Social Sciences and Humanities Research Council of Canada. This book has also been financially assisted by the Province of British Columbia through the British Columbia Heritage Trust and the BC Lottery Fund, and by ongoing support from The Canada Council, the Province of British Columbia Cultural Services Branch, and the Department of Communications of the Government of Canada.

UBC Press
University of British Columbia
6344 Memorial Rd
Vancouver, BC V6T 1Z2
(604) 822-3259
Fax: (604) 822-6083

Contents

Illustrations / vii
Preface / ix

1 The Original People / 3

2 The Arrival of Europeans: Early Contacts / 15

3 Revivalism and Civilization: The Making of a Methodist Missionary / 26

4 Tsimshian Acculturation: 'Religious' Life / 39

5 Tsimshian Acculturation: 'Secular' Life / 61

6 The Role of the Tsimshian in Conversion / 95

Appendix / 113
Notes / 117
Bibliography / 143
Index / 157

Illustrations

Following page 68

1 Port Simpson, 1872. Courtesy British Columbia Archives and Records Service (BCARS), HP10718
2 Methodist church, built in 1876, burnt down in 1932. Courtesy BCARS, HP40471
3 Mission house with church behind, n.d. Courtesy BCARS, HP29023
4 Thomas Crosby with Native woman, 'Queen Victoria,' n.d. Courtesy BCARS, HP665
5 Port Simpson, 1884. Courtesy BCARS, HP10725
6 Panoramic view of Port Simpson, 1884. Courtesy BCARS, HP19666
7 Thomas Crosby and family, Port Simpson, n.d. Courtesy BCARS, HP39063
8 Mission school children and teachers, including girls from Crosby Girls' School and Home, n.d., on church steps. Courtesy BCARS, HP10727
9 Scene at Port Simpson, n.d. Courtesy BCARS, HP632
10 Chief Dudoward's residence, 'Eagle House,' n.d. Courtesy BCARS, HP33952
11 Volunteers at Port Simpson, on beach at Rose Island, n.d. Courtesy BCARS, HP33561
12 Crosby Girls' Home, 1888. Courtesy BCARS, HP39065
13 'Canadian Girls in Training,' Port Simpson, 1890. Courtesy BCARS, HP29028
14 Crosby Girls' Home and School, built in 1892, burnt down in 1921. Courtesy BCARS, HP28997
15 General Hospital, Port Simpson, built in 1892, demolished in 1946. Courtesy BCARS, HP40491

Illustrations

16 Port Simpson totem poles, 1900. Courtesy BCARS, HP14276
17 Hudson's Bay Company boats at Port Simpson on Portland Canal near the Naas River, 1900. Courtesy BCARS, HP50050
18 Thomas Crosby and wife Emma, circa 1914, just before his death. Courtesy BCARS, HP61712
19 Scene from Port Simpson, circa 1915, showing the persistence of Native culture and traditions. Courtesy BCARS, HP88656

Preface

At the end of the fifteenth century, as Europe stood poised at the edge of the modern era, its explorers began venturing westward. Trade routes to the Orient had been blocked and overpopulation pressures gave incentive to adventurous souls to seek new worlds. Although medieval Christian restraints against the unbridled pursuit of wealth were fading, such was not the case with longstanding convictions about the need to convert all nations to 'the gospel of Christ' and to Europe's 'civilized' ways.

The Spanish gave the first indication of how Europeans would deal with aboriginal cultures of the Americas. The Aztec kingdom was plundered and its people forced to convert to Christianity. The motivation and justification for the Spanish conquest of Mexico can best be summarized in the words of Juan Ginés de Sepúlveda. Native people, he said,

> require by their own nature and in their own interests, to be placed under the authority of civilized and virtuous princes or nations, so that they may learn, from the might, wisdom, and law of their conquerors, to practice better morals, worthier customs and a more civilized way of life.
>
> Compare then those blessings enjoyed by the Spaniards ... with those of the homunculi in whom you will scarcely find even vestiges of humanity, who not only possess no science, but who also lack letters ... Neither do they have written laws ... They do not even have private property.
>
> The bringing of iron alone compensates for all the gold and silver taken from America. To ... iron may be added [a long list of agricultural importations]. All these blessings are in addition to writing,

books, culture, excellent laws, and that one supreme benefit which is worth more than all the others combined: the Christian religion.[1]

And so began the history of European expansion into North America.

The French attempted to imitate this Spanish model of conquest in North America when, in 1602, a company was established to trade furs and to build a new, French-Native Catholic nation. Through the efforts of men like Samuel de Champlain and the Catholic orders of the Recollets and Jesuits, they managed to establish a permanent foothold in North America. In 1670, the British followed with the Hudson's Bay Company; however, they never attempted to establish a bi-racial, Christian nation.

The French never realized their ambitions. Initially, settlers were hard to attract, and early traders and priests depended upon Native goodwill and technology for survival. Nonetheless, despite their low numbers, Europeans had a devastating impact on surrounding peoples. The Hurons, for example, were wiped out between 1635 and 1649 because of smallpox, new weapons, alcohol, and conflict with neighbours over the fur resource. Settlers began arriving as furs diminished, and Native peoples were displaced.

This tale would be the norm across what is now Canada. By 1750, the fur trade had moved into the Prairies and into the North. By 1800, only British Columbia would be profitable fur country. European greed for furs resulted in the exhaustion of supplies, necessitating a constant westward search for new sources. Native people inevitably moved westward as well, both to maintain their livelihood and to continue to receive the Western trade items upon which they had come to depend.

European settlement followed fur trade; and settlers and Native people, by and large, could not co-exist. After 1763, British policy in North America was to extinguish Native title and to stake out reserves onto which Native people could move, thereby marginalizing them.

Few Europeans considered the impact of such policies. Among these few who did, however, missionaries stand out. From the Recollet missions in New France to Protestant and Catholic missions in the Maritimes, Upper Canada, the Prairies, and, eventually, in British Columbia, missionaries sought to convert Native people to the twin pillars of Christianity and Western civilization. Typically, they saw only two alternatives for Native peoples: conversion to Western ways or extinction. Maintenance of traditional ways of life was not considered to be an option. Realistically, given the nature of Western ideology and Western views of nature and technology, the missionaries may have been correct in their assumption.

The writing of history, until recently, has usually marginalized Native history. Very typically, allusions are made to traditional Native cultures to show how and when they lost their viability. Materialist writers such as Robin Fisher argue for the decline of Native cultures upon the onset of European settlement, when traditional sources of wealth and livelihood were interrupted because of incompatible land-use philosophies. Ecological analyses, such as that of Calvin Martin, on the other hand, assert that the mere introduction of Western technology, religion, and disease destroyed Native cultures by disrupting and nullifying traditional practices and beliefs.

Neither approach is satisfactory. Neither hears the voices of Native people themselves. There is a simple reason for this omission: virtually all of the evidence left from the period of early contact, including the records of the first anthropologists, is from the European perspective. Missionaries, in particular, were extremely skilled in selling the public their view of the nature of the contact between the two cultures, and the success or failure of missions is still often defined according to missionary terms. Today, even after stripping away the ethnocentricity of the sources, students of contact, whether Native or non-Native, can only conjecture about the mental and spiritual responses of Natives as they encountered Europeans.

Henri Frankfort has postulated that early Middle Eastern cultures did not distinguish between dream and consciousness, myth and reality, subject and object, supernatural and natural, sacred and secular, superstition and science, animate and inanimate, past, present, and future, and so forth.[2] The same applies, in whole or in part, to many North American peoples, and most certainly to the Tsimshian. Hence, because these distinctions are central to the worldview of Europeans, awareness of this fundamental difference between Native and European cultures may be an important clue to the dynamics of contact.

Still, it is extremely difficult to construct reliable images of Native cultures prior to contact. Any Native recollection of their tradition prior to contact would have been influenced by the contact relationship. Hence, it is impossible to develop an image of 'pure' Native cultures in pre-contact times. To this must be added the fact that anthropologists often present Native cultures as static entities which were introduced to concepts of change and time after contact. However, even before contact, similar to cultures all over the globe, Native cultures had changed and evolved.

Perhaps the most fruitful approach to the study of Native response to European intrusion lies in examining the former's reasons for their behaviour towards the latter. Why did they trade? Why didn't they send Europeans away? Why did they accept missionaries? Why did they agree to reservations? Why did alcohol and drug abuse become such severe problems? These questions must be answered from the Native perspective.

Above all, analysis of Native cultures, from the past to the present, must acknowledge that Native people have always lived, and still live, within the context of their own cultures. It is incorrect to say that Native cultures became non-viable or disappeared. Such thinking reflects a paternalism which sees Native cultures as inherently incapable of responding to the complexities of European culture. Native cultures today, although they are the product of a mixture of traditional and European values, are, nonetheless, uniquely Native. Cultures are ever-changing, ever-evolving, and Native cultures are no exception.

This book attempts to answer some questions about the late nineteenth-century Tsimshian response to the Methodist missionary, Thomas Crosby, by examining, as closely as possible, why they acted and reacted as they did. Crosby was a typical nineteenth-century missionary who sought to 'convert and civilize.' Did his mission 'succeed'? Most literature on missions judges success primarily on the basis of whether or not missionaries were able to implement their policies. I suggest that the fate of Crosby's mission work cannot be seen in isolation from the Tsimshian response to that work. In fact, the Tsimshian had invited the Methodist Church to send them a missionary after some of their number had converted to Methodist Christianity while in Victoria in 1873. Furthermore, after Crosby arrived in 1874, he had their co-operation when he demanded that they dismantle traditional housing, abandon their religious practices, destroy their totems, and forsake some of their historic subsistence activities. The Tsimshian acknowledged, in later years, that their acceptance of Crosby's mission work was directly related to a desire to participate in the merging economic, political, and social environment of late nineteenth-century British Columbia. The mission began to experience difficulty when it became obvious that Crosby would not be able to fulfil their desire to find a participatory role in British Columbia society while still remaining Tsimshian. Settlers and, particularly, government administrators, who controlled land policy and legislation (Indian Act, potlatch prohibition, hunting and fishing regulations, etc.), deliberately placed obstacles in the way of Indian self-government and self-expression. Many of the well-documented contemporary symptoms of demoralization, such as substance abuse, suicide, and depression, spring directly from this late nineteenth- and early twentieth-century oppression.

Missionaries, and many historians and anthropologists who have succeeded them, have seen these problems as evidence of an inability on the part of Native people to cope with Western ways. Perhaps the attention which is lavished on uncovering and romanticizing pre-contact Native cultures is simply an attempt to explain why contact was detrimental. As noted above, however, such efforts do not do justice to the reality of Native cultures and actions because they often fail to recognize that these cultures still exist – albeit in a form which includes two hundred years of interaction with White culture. It is not the inability of Native cultures to deal with White culture which is at the root of today's problems. Rather, it is the systematic oppression of the former by the latter.

Hence, analysis of the contact relationship, while being aided by some theorizing on pre-contact cultures, should focus more squarely on the dynamics of contact. Any relationship includes at least two parties and, hence, comprehension of the relationship requires understanding of the motivations, feelings, and rationales of both parties.

In the case of the relationship between the Methodist missionary, Thomas Crosby, and the Port Simpson Tsimshian, it is clear that both parties had aims and goals. And, because Crosby was a lone European in a foreign setting, his ability to do what he wanted depended upon Tsimshian initiative. They had their own reasons for how they lived during the time Crosby resided in their midst.

Although ten years have passed since most of the material in this book was written, recent research on the Tsimshian and on missions merely reinforces and substantiates my contentions. Although I have consulted some of the literature of the last ten years and have made changes to the chapter on Tsimshian culture, the rest of the text is essentially unchanged.

While this book attempts to elucidate Tsimshian reasons for inviting Crosby to be their missionary, and while it evaluates the progress of the ensuing relationship, it does not examine, except in a peripheral way, the syncretic nature of the new forms of life in Port Simpson. There is still a strong need to examine the parallels between Native and European cultural practices, and the elements of continuity and change among the Tsimshian.

I would like to thank Marjorie Halpin for suggesting the importance of looking at Tsimshian reasons for conversion, Hugh Johnston for valuable critical comments, the Union of BC Indian Chiefs for use of their files, Special Collections at UBC, the Provincial Archives, Marilyn Harrison and J.E. Nix for United Church documents, and Jean Wilson of UBC Press for her assistance in putting the project together. In particular, I would like to single out Robin Fisher for his valuable comments and encouragement. I took issue with some aspects of his book, *Contact and Conflict*, and, rather than discouraging my line of thought, he pushed me to present it clearly. Such is scholarship and academic integrity at its best.

CHAPTER ONE

The Original People

When Thomas Crosby began his missionary work at Fort Simpson in 1874, the Tsimshian had been in contact with Europeans for almost one hundred years. This contact, mainly with Russian, British, American, and Canadian fur traders, and with the Church Missionary Society missionary William Duncan, had introduced them to cultures which differed radically from their own.

Duncan was typical of most European missionaries in that he saw non-Western aboriginal societies as primitive forms of civilization which would inevitably give way to the superiority of Western ways. Such missionaries usually failed to recognize that other cultures were as complex as were their own, and that non-Western people were also capable of dealing with and resolving such universal human paradoxes as joy and sorrow, life and death, happiness and pain, and hunger and plenty. This failure, in addition to their inability to see that their notion of the superiority of Christian civilization was merely a construct of their own cultural bias rather than an objective, God-ordained truth, explains, to a large extent, the nature of missionary/Native relations. To understand the dynamic of missionary/Tsimshian relations it is necessary, first of all, to establish a clear picture of the nature of Tsimshian culture and the results of contact with European culture prior to the arrival of Thomas Crosby.

Immediately, the historian and student of this relationship is faced with a grave difficulty. What exactly was the nature of Tsimshian culture prior to the arrival of Europeans? Being non-literate people, the Tsimshian did not leave written accounts of their past. Traditions were transmitted orally, giving the culture a fluidity, in which past and present were commingled. In addition, as with all cultures, new influences constantly modified Native lifestyles.

Hence, when Franz Boas, the first serious recorder of Tsimshian ceremonies, myths, traditions, and social patterns (and our principle source of information about traditional Tsimshian culture), began his work in the late nineteenth century, he was transcribing information about a people who had been in contact with Europeans (including missionaries, such as Duncan and Crosby) for over a hundred years. As one anthropologist has noted: 'An expanding economy, a declining population and missionary and government directives all exacted changes in traditional ceremonies. The late nineteenth century also witnessed new ceremonies, emergent as part of the acculturation process.'[1] The problem of time is compounded by the fact that one of the other major sources of information about the Tsimshian, Marius Barbeau, was highly critical of Boas's methods of acquiring and recording information.[2] Besides the studies of Boas and Barbeau, there was little collecting and analyzing of information concerning Tsimshian culture.[3]

Nonetheless, while it may be difficult to obtain a total picture of pre-contact Tsimshian culture, there were, undoubtedly, at the time of the early anthropologists, distinct continuities with the past – continuities which can shed light on traditional ways of living, being, and thinking. Indeed, continuities extend right to the present.

It is useful to borrow Clifford Geertz's distinction between 'culture,' which he defines as 'ordered systems of meaning and symbols, in terms of which social interaction takes place,' and social systems, that is, '[the] pattern of social interaction itself.'[4]

> On one level there is the framework of beliefs, expressive symbols, and values in terms of which individuals define their world, express their feelings, and make their judgments; on the other level there is the ongoing process of interactive behaviour, whose persistent form we call social structure. Culture is the fabric of meaning in terms of which human beings interpret their experience and guide their action; social structure is the form that action takes, the actually existing network of social relations.[5]

This is a most useful distinction. What people believe, their values and their world-views, are distinguished from the environment in which they occur, namely, their social networks. Ideally, values and world-views will be reflected in social structures. But it may happen that everyday social patterns are completely at odds with cultural values (e.g., high divorce rates and many single parent families in a culture that holds marriage as a supreme value). This may be particularly true when social and cultural environments experience outside influences, causing world-views and actual social behaviour to diverge from one another.[6]

With regard to the Tsimshian, much of the early literature concentrated on the social structure, particularly on rank and on the potlatch, while 'beliefs,' 'symbols,' and 'values' (i.e., culture) have only recently been studied and interpreted. To understand more fully the impact of contact, a knowledge of both facets of Tsimshian society is essential.

The Tsimshian lived in the valleys and territories between the Nass and Skeena rivers and from the Pacific coast to a point as far west as the convergence of the Bulkley and Skeena rivers. Their highly developed social structure, elaborate ceremonial life and mythology, wide range of artistic skills, and effective management of natural resources were evidence of one of the most complex North American Native societies. Native people speaking the Tsimshian language were divided into three dialect groups: The Tsimshian Proper, who lived around the mouth of the Skeena; the Gitksan, whose villages were on the Upper Skeena; and the Nishga of the Nass Valley. Each dialect group was divided into several distinct groupings or villages, of which there were originally ten among the Coast Tsimshian, each in turn divided into four phratries: eagle, raven, wolf, and killer whale.

The phratry, which cut across village boundaries, was the primary unit of social order. It regulated spouse selection by requiring marriage outside of one's phratry. Tsimshian society was matrilineal (not matriarchal), that is, inheritance and status were passed to the father's oldest sister's son. Boys belonged to their mother's phratry and left home at the age of nine or ten to live with maternal uncles and to take up membership in their mother's phratry.[7] Inheritance along these lines of kinship determined how a person was to conduct his life: what social class he belonged to, what position of rank he could attain, where he could live, whom he could marry, where he could hunt and fish, what crests he could use, and so on.[8] Each village contained a representative group from each phratry, and this unit was known as a lineage or household group, the most elementary living unit among the Tsimshian.[9] The members of such a unit included a male head, brothers, maternal cousins and sister's sons, and their wives and daughters and were ranked from chief down. The lineage group, with the chief as custodian, jointly held rights to food processing areas. It possessed its own houses and campsites as well as a number of privileges: ceremonial titles, totem poles, ceremonial paraphernalia, crests, ritual performances, and the right to relate and dramatize the legends and myths concerning the ancestral origins of their group. The lineage group co-operated socially and ceremonially as an independent unit and created a sense of community based on a common female ancestor (grandmother). The main link to a phratry other than one's own was through the father. 'It is along this social structural line that the services and phratry interactions of the potlatch take place.'[10]

From February to October the lineage group was highly mobile. In February, it moved to traditional household sites on the Nass to fish for eulachon. Each family unit had its own canoe, fishing equipment, shelter, and fire but moved, with the rest of the group, under the supervision of the house head. From March to June, the people fished for salmon at traditional sites further up the Nass. During the summer and early fall, they broke up into small units to dry the salmon and gather berries for winter use. Besides gathering for their own use, these groups gathered extra for the feasting and potlatching of the winter season. During the winter months, from November to February, the Tsimshian put aside their gathering, hunting, and fishing activities, and potlatching and feasting occupied most of their time. This was also the time when the spirits became active. The forces and questions which had to be dealt with at this time gave the Tsimshian ample opportunity to utilize their great musical, artistic, and dramatic abilities – talents which would later make Crosby's revivalistic brand of Methodism attractive to them.

In the winter villages, each lineage group had its own house, generally large enough to contain all the members of the group. Each house could contain up to forty or fifty people and was one of several lined up above the high tide water-line along the beach. The village was essentially a conglomeration of lineage groups with a representative from each phratry and was considered the permanent home of each group. Each of the Coast Tsimshian villages had chosen a separate winter village site on the islands flanking Metlakatla Pass. The chief of the highest ranking lineage group was considered the head of the village. As with the lineage group, the village possessed its own crests, totems, houses, and ceremonies. Most of the characteristics of the lineage group and its head defined, on a larger scale, the nature of the village and the role of its chief.[11]

The chief decided on times to travel to the fishing and hunting areas, administered village property, supervised slaves, organized defence, and gave potlatches. His power was theoretically limited by the village council, consisting of the other lineage group heads. Although potlatches were given by individual lineage groups, the council organized them and also advised the chief in the selection of wives, organized the building of his houses, decided on how village wealth should be apportioned, and, generally, gave him permission for any extensive undertakings.[12]

Rank was clearly defined in Tsimshian society,[13] a fact that has led some to argue for the existence of class divisions.[14] Philip Drucker, however, has argued that Tsimshian society did not contain classes but was divided in terms of 'graded statuses'; no two people were ranked in exactly the same manner but each had a grading relative to the next.[15] Wilson Duff distinguishes three classes – nobles, commoners, and slaves – but then hastens to add that among the people there was a 'graded series of positions of rank.'[16] Whatever the case, rank and status were of vital importance to the Tsimshian.

Rank and status were closely connected to the inter-relationship between heredity and wealth. Rank and status were usually inherited, while the acquisition of wealth demonstrated and reinforced the prestige of the chief and his group. The potlatch regulated this phenomenon and demonstrated the right of an individual to the position or title being inherited or granted.

The potlatch is one of the more well-known and discussed features of Northwest Coast Native life. Yet, its purpose is widely debated. Ecological, functional/structural, psychological, symbolic, and other theoretical approaches have been employed to try to interpret what the potlatch meant to those who used it. This renders understanding difficult. Nonetheless, some aspects of the potlatch are clear. At a potlatch, the guests and relatives of the giver would gather, and the host would provide feasts and distribute property in amounts that varied according to the rank of the recipient. There were mortuary potlatches, which were held as memorial services for dead chiefs; installation potlatches, in which the dead chief's names, songs, crests, dances, powers, and properties were passed to his successor; initiation potlatches for secret societies and acquisition of spirit power; potlatches to wipe out insults of shame; war potlatches; and life-crisis feasts.

The giving of potlatches necessitated the gathering of provisions beyond the primary needs of food, clothing, and shelter. Each lineage group co-operated in the accumulation of goods, and the quality of the feast and the amount of goods distributed contributed to the leader's and group's status. This fact has led some to conclude that 'the prime purpose of Indian wealth was display and ostentatious consumption to demonstrate prosperity and power to others, thus enhancing the local group's prestige.'[17] Furthermore, 'the potlatch system was responsible for much of the emphasis on wealth ownership, both individual and group. The necessity for goods to be used in potlatching was a stimulus which motivated individuals to produce and acquire as much as possible.'[18] Wealth, according to this view, validated a person's (and his or her group's) claim to certain rank and status as well as the whole system of ranking. The distribution also validated the social rank of the guest group as reflected in seating arrangements, use of titles, and order of gift giving.

This essentially 'secular' explanation of the potlatch, however, fails to do justice to its complexity. It looks at social function without paying heed to cultural values and world-view. Drucker has pointed out that

> when a title was concerned, the announcement included an account of its origin, how it had been acquired by an ancestor, whether bestowed by a supernatural being or captured in warfare, how it had been transmitted down the family line to the person on whom it was being bestowed. Much of the legendary history of the group was recited to prove the right to use the name or privilege.[19]

All events accompanied by a potlatch involved this recapitulation of the origins of the occasion for celebration. The present was linked to the time of 'beginnings.' Irving Goldman has noted that, in Kwakiutl lineage succession 'what was inherited was not a quantity of power, but the right to represent an ancestral or supernatural being.'[20] Rank was determined by divine fiat, and is 'specifically the holy order of the founding ancestors, a primary order of existence that cannot change without grave disruption.'[21] The same was true for the Tsimshian. Myth tied the present to the time of origins 'to bring the powers taking part in it back to life ... [and] to make their power once more effective.'[22] The name of a person was central to the system of ranking. As hereditary property, it clearly defined the place of the individual and carried with it a particular social valuation based on its origin and the honour or disrepute of previous bearers. The name indicated, at feasts and potlatches, the status of the bearer as well as all the material and ceremonial rights to which he or she was entitled. For chiefs, the inherited names also signified their relationship to the non-human or spirit beings encountered by the original holders of those names.[23]

Goldman explains the importance of names:

> Each new generation reconstitutes on earth that primordial state when the founders were just moving out of their non-human and non-earthly realms. This primordial state, like that of birth, invokes the great powers of emergence, of transformation, and of initiation. To be connected through lineage with the Beginnings is to be in touch with the genera-

tive powers of birth, more fundamentally with the original sources of human creation. Thus the inheritance of names of a lineage is no mere social transmission of membership, it is rather a ritual process ... that serves to maintain and periodically to strengthen the ties between present generations and their earlier formative state.[24]

Thus, the inheritance of names entailed a spiritual transformation: the 'ancestral being leaves one human carrier to be reincarnated in another.'[25] At any event involving the distribution of goods 'the giver is privileged to be the god-like source of valued treasures and powers. Powers were first granted in the primary (mythical) era to ancestors who transmitted them to their heirs.[26] It should be noted that, among the Tsimshian, there is indeed some indication of a belief in reincarnation.[27]

At the cultural level, the level of world-view and values, the potlatch provided its participants with a sense of belonging, a link to their origins, and some understanding of the meaning of life. Along with an elaborate array of winter ceremonies, it defined their world, focused their feelings and values, and placed their actions in a meaningful context. At the level of social structure, the potlatch gave order to everyday behaviour and provided a structural framework in which to work out daily social interactions and interrelationships.

Thus, the significance of wealth and status must be seen in the wider context of both cultural values and social patterns rather than as ends in and of themselves.

It is also in the context of cultural meaning that the so-called 'religious life' of Native people must be examined. In Western traditions, a sharp delineation is often drawn between 'religious' and 'secular.' Goldman argues that Northwest Coast Native people made no such distinction. About the Kwakiutl, he writes, 'Their concept of what we call sacred does not ... encompass their religion. It refers only to the presence of powers and spirits that require appropriate human response.'[28] The opening statement of the Gitksan and Wet'suwet'en land claim in the British Columbia Supreme Court makes the same point when it notes that feasts were at once 'political, legal, economic, social, spiritual, ceremonial, and educational.'[29]

While it may be useful to say that Native people treated all of life as sacred, there are nonetheless specific activities and states, such as rites, ceremonies, doctrines, myth, and worship, that are distinct from other activities and states. (A worshipful trance, for example, is qualitatively different from hunting deer or fishing.) These activities are what we call religion, and they integrate life's experiences and contradictions into a meaningful and coherent relationship which assumes both purpose and direction. Geertz notes that 'sacred symbols function to synthesize a people's ethos – the tone, character and quality of their life, its moral and aesthetic style and mood – and their world-view – the picture they have of the way things in sheer actuality are, their most comprehensive ideas of order.'[30] Religion is, thus, distinguished from culture. If culture is the world-view, the fundamental values of meaning 'in terms of which human beings interpret their experience and guide their action,'[31] then religion is the network of symbols and myths which give tangible expression to the cultural foundation and make it real. Religion, like the social system, is a reflection of the world-view and values by which people live.

One of the major components of traditional Tsimshian religion was their mythology. While it dealt with such matters as social structure, everyday life, taboos, ceremonies, and rituals, it also gave the Tsimshian explanations for the present state of the world: 'The action of myths took place in an age of supernaturals and semi-divine ancestors before the present features and social customs of the world were fully established.'[32] Myths thus connected past and present in such a way as to make the latter comprehensible. They provided a prototype for society as well as an archetype for appropriate behaviour.

As noted earlier, lineage succession feasts and potlatches required the recitation of the myth describing the origins of the lineage. The original encounter with non-humans was dramatized, and the people identified with the lineage which was formed at that time, using crests to show what their ancestors had seen and heard. The whole complex passed down from generation to generation. Mircea Eliade argues that the 'sacred time' in which a person is placed by re-enacting the original experience is not a matter of impersonation but is an actual reinvolvement with the 'in-the-beginning' moment. The ritual which is undertaken for the re-enactment 'abolished profane, chronological time and [recovered] the sacred time of myth. Man [became] contemporary with the exploits that the gods performed *in illo tempore.*'[33] Whether or not Eliade's analysis is correct, it seems fair to say that ritual involvement with myth meant, for the Tsimshian, an intimate spiritual connection with the sources of that ritual as well as a sense of transcendence over everyday routine.

In addition to detailing the origin of the present order of the world and giving prescriptions for the conduct of life, myth also provided the 'sacred' context which made this knowledge effective. Rites, taboo, prayers, and ceremonies were visible expressions of the ideals of mythology and gave purpose to the carrying out of everyday activities.

At the heart of the system of rites and taboos that guided everyday life was the relationship between the Tsimshian and the environment – which was alive in the fullest sense of the word. The forces of nature, plants, animals, spirit beings, ghosts, and what we would call supernatural beings shared their existence with people, and their co-operation and assistance was vital to successful living. Elaborate rituals and strong taboos were thought to preserve this relationship.

An important group of such rituals centred around the guardian-spirit quest and the so-called 'life-crisis observances.'[34] These crisis observances corresponded to the physiological changes occurring during the person's life cycle: birth, puberty, and death as well as other less sharply defined stages. At such stages, a person was particularly vulnerable to evil influences and only by means of carefully prepared steps was he or she able to overcome the crisis and move on to the next stage of life. Purification was central to this carefully observed program because the person, at the moment of crisis, was unclean to the supernatural beings. Purification had to be accompanied by ritual acts appropriate to the occasion:

> While many persons and things might be affected by an individual in one of these critical states, fish and game were considered more susceptible. Fresh fish and all meats were tabu to the person, and diet was limited to old dry fish. Seclusion, out of sight of the fishermen and hunters, was the rule ... and even approaching a salmon stream was forbidden.[35]

Once the crisis had been overcome, a potlatch would be held to announce publicly the new status of this individual.

The relationship to what we call the natural environment required appropriate responses as well. In fact, rather than the Western distinction between the natural and the supernatural, the Tsimshian distinguished between human and non-human beings. They saw humans as part of an 'interacting continuum which includes animals and spirits.'[36] Each can influence the course of events in the realm of the other. Animals, birds, and fish have villages 'where they appear in human form and live, work, and converse in a human way.'[37] 'For the Tsimshian, animals are not alien beings. They are, in fact "people." Because animals are people, they understand reciprocity in the same way people do.'[38] The relationship is so close that transformations occur regularly. As Marjorie Halpin notes, 'a person wearing a crest headdress raised and lowered his or her head, becoming successively human/animal/human/animal.'[39]

To use waters, exploit natural resources, hunt animals, or fish for eulachon and salmon, therefore, appropriate preparation and ritual purification were necessary. At the heart of this preparation was the asking of permission from each exploited element of nature or animal for its use. This would be followed by training, which made the person acceptable to the giver. The spirits of each 'being' had to be placated, and, to this end, the first salmon, eulachon, tree, and so on was treated ceremonially, ensuring that it would be available for future use. Strict taboos surrounded this event, and exploitation or violation of taboos had grave consequences, the most serious of which would be the spirit's withdrawal from the life of the people, resulting in the absence of that particular resource, animal, or plant.[40] 'Animals were killed, or allowed themselves to be killed, to supply food and other benefits to mankind. Rites were performed atoning for the deed and acknowledging man's dependence on the supernaturals.'[41] Closely related to this response to non-human beings was the winter ceremonial complex, particularly the four dancing societies: the Cannibals, the Dog-eaters, the Destroyers, and the Firethrowers. Marjorie Halpin described the Tsimshian winter in the following way:

> Winter brought the 'time of taboos' and people moved back into their winter great cedar plank houses in permanent 'totem pole' or winter villages to wait again for spring. This was the ritual season, the time when the spirits came down from the mountain to lurk in the forests surrounding the villages. Certain houses were sanctified for the season by placing sacred rings of red cedar bark on the doors; inside, the members of the dancing societies initiated new members, and people possessed by the Cannibal and Dog-eater spirits roamed the woods.[42]

Winter ended the fishing, hunting, and gathering of the milder seasons, and, because of the topography and wet climate of the region, a great deal of time was spent indoors. The contrast between the two periods of time brought to a focus the relationship between human and non-human beings.

As already noted, because the people had to seek the goodwill of the species they had 'used' for their sustenance, they observed rites and taboos to ensure these species' return. These beings had given themselves to people voluntarily. The exchange was, therefore, one-sided; people received the life of other beings who died for them so that they could live. But they had not given their lives in return.

This imbalance necessitated reciprocity. The shaman acted as the 'transformer' in the life cycle, and it was his or her personal mission to enter the 'vale of death,' and, by returning, demonstrate that reversal was possible: 'The shamanic "technique of ecstasy" ... is appropriate to the mission of reversing the life cycle by going outside the normal boundaries of life.'[43] In the Cannibal society, for example, the member (symbolically) leaves the human world to meet the cannibal spirit, receive its power, and then is brought back safely and restored to the normal human state by the shaman.

Both the Tsimshian and Kwakiutl, whose beliefs about the relationship between human and non-human life, particularly animal life, were similar,[44] believed that, during the winter ceremonies, the spirits' 'summer is the earth winter, so that they are always in their winter dances when they appear among human beings [who are in their earth summer].'[45] Katerina S. Reid, in her analysis of Kwakiutl winter feasts, has attached the idea of the need for reciprocity to this seasonal relationship. The summer life of the people 'confronts them with an ethical problem they cannot solve: they find themselves destroying beings they reverence in order to sustain their lives, and so contract a debt to the animals under the laws of necessity.'[46] This tension could be resolved in two ways: 'a symbolic solution consisting of a scheme of guilt and amendment, and a psychological solution consisting of an effective inversion.'[47] The animals, who gave themselves freely to humans in the summer, 'turn hunters in the winter with men as their game ... If men give themselves voluntarily to these animal spirits to be killed and eaten, they can repay the debt of the summer.'[48] This reversal removed the debt, as each party had given of itself freely in the appropriate season, and, thus, people removed their guilt for doing violence to their friends, whom they paradoxically had to kill to survive. The emphasis was on the voluntary nature of giving, for the 'act of passivity' on the part of humans not only made amends for what they had to do to survive but it also gave them the gift of 'spiritual life.'[49]

Recently, Margaret Seguin has noted that

> in addition to the Tsimshian tribes and other human groups with which they were acquainted, Tsimshian recognized other societies. Each animal species had its own village, with 'Real People,' commoners and slaves, similar to Tsimshian villages. Food came to the Tsimshian by the animals' own consent, directed by their chiefs. There were also villages for human ghosts, with similar social structure ... Actions taken on animal bodies in human villages influenced animals in

their own villages. Complete, respectful consumption of animal bodies was required to ensure the health of the animals ... The consequences of actions in one domain could be observed in the others. Real animals in their villages were aware of actions taken by humans; human shamans were especially adept at perceiving other worlds.[50]

The need for reciprocity and similar 'spiritual' questions challenged the Tsimshian to the limits of their creativity, resulting in sophisticated art forms and elaborate and dramatic performances, in which the relationship between human and other beings played a major role. All Tsimshian attempts to bring order and coherence to their world clearly showed that their world-view was integrated with everyday activities, and that it provided some degree of resolution to perplexing problems and questions of meaning. Dramatic performances, music, mythology, and religion objectified these conflicts and resolutions in a manner which satisfied the deepest needs of the people. The social system was a direct outgrowth, and reflection, of cultural values, and the two formed an integrated whole.

In the late eighteenth century, the coherence and integration of Tsimshian culture was challenged by the coming of a people with a radically different cultural basis – a challenge that would eventually lead the Tsimshian to decide to move from their own cultural heritage and to adopt the patterns of these newcomers.

CHAPTER TWO

The Arrival of Europeans: Early Contacts

Sometime after 1774, nine Coast Tsimshian villages, apparently already famous for their trading skills, especially with the Haida, Tlingit, Nishga, and Gitksan,[1] established relations with a new group of traders – the Europeans. In 1792, the Spanish explorer, Jacinto Caamano, spent a month among the Coast Tsimshian. The familiarity and readiness with which they received him and the metal buttons they wore indicated that they had made previous contact with Europeans,[2] probably Russians, Americans, and British. These contacts had more than likely enabled them to consolidate their previous trading power by preventing the inland Natives from trading directly with the Europeans.

Little is known about Tsimshian trade with Europeans up until 1828. In that year, Sir George Simpson, governor of the Hudson's Bay Company, in an effort to establish a British monopoly on trade with the Northwest Coast Natives, decided that the time was ripe to build a fort just south of the Russian boundary in order to block American and Russian access to the furs collected in the area. By the end of 1830, a site was chosen inland on the Nass River, and Fort Nass was opened in 1831.

Pressure from both Company traders and Natives led the Hudson's Bay Company to search for a new site. Traders found Fort Nass unattractive because it was miles inland from the heavy trading activity of the coast, thus giving the Americans and Russians a trading advantage and rendering the fort unprofitable. In addition, it contained no sheltered anchorage. The Coast Tsimshian disliked it because they faced stiff trading competition from the inland Tsimshian and Tlingit. One of the Coast chiefs, Legaic, who had given his daughter in marriage to Dr. John Kennedy (a physician and leading trader at Fort Nass) in order to consolidate a trading alliance between his tribe and the Company, offered the latter one of his camping areas as a new fort site. Fort Simpson was the result, established in 1834, just south of the Russian boundary and right at the mouth of the Nass River.

The other eight Coast Tsimshian villages, which wintered along Metlakatla Pass, responded quickly to this change by moving their winter villages to Fort Simpson and forming 'a loose sort of confederacy, although the individual tribes never quite gave up their autonomy.'[3] In addition to this physical realignment, the social structure was also altered – the major change being the emergence of a series of powerful chiefs named Legaic. Indeed, there is evidence which suggests that Legaic had been consolidating his power before the establishment of Fort Simpson.[4] His daughter's marriage to Kennedy had enhanced his role as a trader, and he became middleman for many Native people to trade with the Company. In 1836, a smallpox epidemic led to an increase in potlatching, as young men sought to gain positions opened up due to premature deaths. Many leaders were impoverished in their attempts to match the potlatches given by wealthy new traders such as Legaic. Legaic's status increased dramatically as he gave tremendous potlatches – potlatches which other chiefs were incapable of matching. On account of this wealth, and through alleged trickery, warfare, and trade monopolies, he became the leading chief at Fort Simpson – a position he maintained until well after William Duncan's arrival in the mid-1850s.[5]

Relations between Native people and traders, although not always amicable, were generally conducive to trade.[6] Bad relations would have negated the purpose for which each was using the other. There were occasional anxious moments, but, generally, the anxiety was the result of Natives feuding amongst themselves. Traditional rivalries between the Tsimshian, Haida, and Tlingit needed only the smallest spark to ignite into violence, and the fact that all came to Fort Simpson to trade with the Company increased the likelihood of conflict. Liquor was also often a factor leading to hostilities. By the time of the establishment of Fort Simpson, the Natives had acquired a taste for alcohol, and often used it in their potlatching and feasting. During the early years of the fort, liquor was an important trade item, and the Natives often played off the Americans against the Hudson's Bay Company for the cheapest price. In 1842, the Company cancelled all trade in liquor because of its effect on Native ability to collect furs.

During the Hudson's Bay Company years, the Tsimshian maintained their reputation as shrewd bargainers, playing the market and trading with those who offered them the best deal. This state of affairs prompted one of the traders, John Work, to complain: 'It is annoying in the extreme to see the advantage which the black vagabonds endeavour to make of this circumstance.'[7] After the Company ended trade in liquor, it became increasingly difficult for it to compete with the Americans, as the Natives would often hold on to their furs and wait for American ships.[8] While the Hudson's Bay Company always realized what it considered to be reasonable returns for its efforts, there is no question that the presence of American ships continued to drain Company profits throughout the 1840s and 1850s, and the liquor obtained from the Americans continued to exacerbate tensions between different groups of Natives. In 1852, William McNeill reported that the Americans 'threw a large quantity of goods into the market, and kept the Natives from hunting or exciting themselves to obtain fur.'[9] In 1854, the Tsimshian began going to Victoria to trade their furs. From these furs and from prostitution they obtained large amounts of liquor, and, by 1860, Victoria had become so popular that virtually all furs gathered by the Tsimshian were taken there.

Despite the instability of the fur trade, the relationship between the two parties was essentially peaceful, and Native people were often employed by the traders to load ships and tend gardens. The only hostilities were the product of what the traders perceived to be petty acts of vandalism: stealing of pickets from fences, wrecking gardens, shooting off guns, and the like. Liquor was often the cause of such acts and prompted Work, in 1835, to complain about its effects: 'Even with the best of them we don't know the moment a quarrel may arise and even bloodshed may be the result.'[10] Vandalism often tempted the traders to use force, but no record or tradition of violent confrontation survives. In fact, in 1852, the Tsimshian were responsible for preventing the burning down of Fort Simpson.

The fur traders made no attempt to 'direct' change in Native society. Rather, according to Jean Usher, contact 'enhanced the existing cultural forms [because] the aboriginal culture was largely oriented to the acquisition and display of wealth, and the influx of prestige goods from the traders only gave vitality to already existing cultural institutions.'[11] Few new skills were needed, and arts, crafts, housebuilding, and ceremonial life flourished. The move to Fort Simpson, with the resulting social readjustment, and the smallpox epidemic of 1836 made for trying times, but, she argues, Native 'laws still functioned, and by potlatching intensively, they were trying to adjust their real situation to their social ideals ... this was still an Indian dominated society, and the Indian solutions for these problems could still be applied.'[12] Robin Fisher agrees and has stated that the fur trade was a 'mutually beneficial symbiosis in which neither gained from the hostility of the other.' Native people exercised 'a large degree of choice' about what they accepted from European culture, and, hence, the effect on their own culture was 'creative rather than destructive.'[13]

Philip Drucker cautions us about adopting such easy analyses: 'It is not the mere listing of culture items added or subtracted that is significant but the cultural processes and psychological factors involved.'[14] These elements are much harder to isolate. In an interaction such as that between the traders and the Tsimshian, Native social structure continued to function very much along traditional lines. Strains in values and attitudes would not necessarily be immediately reflected in alterations to social systems.

The nature of the fur trade illustrates this well. Trade occupied an ever increasing portion of Tsimshian time. They spent less time hunting, fishing, and gathering for their basic needs, trading instead with other Native groups for fur, meat, fish, and potatoes, which they in turn traded with Whites for whatever goods they desired.[15] By the late 1850s, the Tsimshian spent most of their traditional hunting summer trading in Victoria. Furthermore, with the increase in wealth and depopulation by disease, potlatches and feasts, on a scale never before witnessed, dominated their winter months. Many of these occasions deteriorated to mere ostentatious displays of wealth, destruction of large quantities of goods, or insults to guests in speech and song. There were also challenge feasts, the sole purpose of which was to humiliate guests by providing them with more food and often more rum than they could consume. These feasts have been called 'rivalry potlatches,' and they often provided the occasion for bitter confrontations between rivals for social status.[16] Rather than being a source of order and stability, the potlatch increasingly functioned as an instrument of division.

The mentality required for the fur trade was also at variance with the traditional Tsimshian relationship with non-human beings and violated many of the old taboos. In 1843, the *Fort Simpson Post Journal* reported that the Tsimshian were not bringing in enough fish and added that 'the reason they assign for it, is their having brought them so early to the Fort, they superstitiously imagine our mode of cooking them is the cause of falling off.'[17] The traders were astounded that the Tsimshian did not realize that the school of fish had simply passed, 'they being so tenacious of their own superstitious beliefs.'[18] The desire for European goods required behaviour that conflicted with ancient taboos and rituals. Between 1810 and 1820, sea otter pelts became increasingly difficult to obtain, and Hudson's Bay Company records, throughout the whole era of the fur trade, indicate a steady decline in both number and quality of furs for most species. Undoubtedly, the decline of species produced, for Native people, many inner conflicts.

The winter ceremonial complex became 'secularized' as well. Careful rehearsal of spirit possession and theatrical gimmickry became the order of the day. The increase in wealth and depopulation by disease were partly responsible for this change. If Reid's analysis of the winter ceremonies is correct, it would have been increasingly difficult for Native people to avoid being hypocritical about what they were saying concerning the animal spirits. According to Reid, Native peoples' chief problem with the fur trade era was not in coming to terms with the new wealth but in handling it in such a way that old communal patterns would still be operative. Indeed, the overkilling of animals brought in large amounts of new wealth. But overkilling was a crime, and

> prayers show ... it is the most certain way of making the animals use their equilibrating power and bring illness and death. There is no doubt that illness and death accompanied the new wealth ... The dilemma in which men are involved in their relation to the outside world, represented in the prayers as the problem of the double nature of the animals, and, correspondingly, of man's double desire, was therefore a particularly acute issue at that time.[19]

Indeed, overkilling was seen by most North American Native people as a sure guarantee of retribution. Calvin Martin has suggested that the close relationship between human and other beings was characteristic of all North American hunter-gatherer societies. The non-human world was not seen as a mere aggregate of exploitable resources, but, rather, there was 'genuine kinship and often affection for wildlife and plant-life' and, hence, respect and concern for their welfare. Human and other beings were bound by a compact, and fulfilled each other's needs.[20] Hunting required certain rites and taboos so that the spirit of the being giving its life would not be offended. Failure to follow correct prescriptions could lead to the withdrawal of the offended spirit's species from the area, lack of success for the hunter, and/or the onset of disease. With the coming of Europeans, Native people saw a way to make traditional goals more attainable. The intensification of contact, however, brought disease to the people and a depletion of animals. Traditional shamanic remedies failed to work against these new forces, which were seen as the revenge of the animal-spirits who had been offended by improper preparation for hunting. In turn, Native people in the fur-trading areas retaliated by slaughtering the vindictive species in the hope of rendering their revenge ineffective. Thus began the exploitive fur trade in which Native people eagerly gathered furs for the Europeans. According to Martin:

> By accepting the European material culture, the Natives were impelled to accept the European abstract culture, especially the European religion. The result was that their own spiritual beliefs were subverted as they abandoned their implements for those of the white man. Native spiritual beliefs lost not only their practical effectiveness, in part owing to the replacement of the traditional magical and animistic view of nature by the monotheistic and exploitive European view, but they were no longer necessary as a source of definition and theoretical support for the new Europe-derived material culture. Western technology, in a word, made more 'sense' if it was accompanied by western religion: Christianity.[21]

Disease, European trade, and, eventually, Christianity, concludes Martin, led to apostasy, the most obvious sign of change being the unrestricted slaughter of certain game.

Whether or not Martin's analysis fully explains the fur trade, it is certain that, for the Tsimshian, collecting surpluses of furs for the Europeans did not harmonize easily with fundamental beliefs, particularly those expressed in the winter ceremonials. The sacred symbols could no longer provide their original meaning, and this explains, in part, the staged dramatic presentations and extravagant displays of the mid-nineteenth century. Thus, while certain social forms appeared to remain operative, some underlying presuppositions were challenged at a fundamental level.

At about the time the Tsimshian began to go to Victoria, another agent of social change, one which would attempt to 'direct' alterations in Tsimshian society and accelerate the despiritualization begun by the fur trade, appeared at Fort Simpson. William Duncan, representing the (Anglican) Church Missionary Society, began his long and famous career on the Northwest Coast in 1857. English by birth, Duncan had risen, through persistence and hard work, from a poor working class background to the lower middle class of Victorian England. His Christianity was strongly evangelical, emphasizing the total depravity and worthlessness of humanity. This emphasis had led Duncan, as it had so many other evangelical missionaries, to a dramatic conversion from a highly exaggerated state of sinfulness. These 'marvellous deliverances' often gave such people a heightened sense of responsibility for other 'lost souls,' and the missionary vocation was a popular way to exercise this responsibility. In addition to presenting the gospel, missionaries such as Duncan sought to reproduce the society and institutions of Victorian England among their converts. In their minds, they saw England as the greatest nation on earth, paramount because it had risen out of the bondage of paganism through the liberating message of the gospel. They saw it as their duty to spread, to all corners of the world, both Christianity and an idealized form of the civilized life of England, complete with Victorian notions of work, leisure, clothing, sex roles, housing, furniture, and education.[22] Everyday life and the gospel were inseparable.

Duncan attempted to present this two-fold gospel at Fort Simpson. The skill manifested in Tsimshian arts persuaded him that these were people capable of 'improvement,' but he was appalled by the feasting and winter ceremonials that reflected the religious beliefs which he wished to replace. The wasteful potlatches, drunkenness, prostitution, and violence of Tsimshian life convinced him of the unsuitability of Native ways in an emerging European society. The disastrous results of contact proved, to Duncan, that heathen ways could not cope with those of the Europeans, and that only Christianity could act as a mediating force which would enable the Native people to survive.

Indeed, these were critical years for the Tsimshian. By 1860, the Hudson's Bay Company had lost virtually all trade to Victoria because of that city's easy money and available liquor. Hamilton Moffatt, a Company man, complained that if the Natives were 'kept well under the hands of the law at Victoria, they would not be so desirous to migrate.'[23] In 1860, he broke Company policy by giving the Natives liquor in order to attract more furs, and, in the following year, the Company raised fur prices substantially – all to no avail.

The winter seasons of 1859-60 and 1860-1 were difficult for both the fur traders and Duncan. There was continual fighting and drunkenness during the winter feasting and ceremonies as well as feuding with the Haida. From September 1859 to May 1860, according to Company officials, three men and four women were killed during drunken fights. In June of 1860, Duncan's house was plundered. In February of 1862, as many were leaving for Victoria, the *Fort Simpson Post Journal* reported that 'a larger number than usual of females are going to prostitute themselves.'[24]

At the same time, Duncan established roots among the Tsimshian by opening a school and teaching the children reading, writing, arithmetic, singing, and religion. Between July 1861 and July 1862, 58 Indians were baptized (37 men and 21 children), of whom 22 were under 20 years of age, 27 between 20 and 30, 5 between 30 and 40, and 4 over 40.[25] Duncan's success was modest, and there were no mass conversions. Very early, he toyed with the idea of moving himself and his followers from Fort Simpson to escape the unsettled conditions.

Why was there so little positive response to his efforts? Jean Usher notes the following:

> Before 1857, contact with Whites was on a regular, ordered basis. The Tsimshian appeared to be in control of their own society, and were coping remarkably well with the effects of guns, liquor and disease introduced by European civilization. Their reaction to a missionary who denied the basis of their society was not that of a disoriented people. The Tsimshian neither capitulated to Duncan's ideas, nor made any hysterical attacks on the missionary as a last defence of their old disintegrating values. The Tsimshian were curious about Duncan's ideas, as they were about many European ways.[26]

Their isolation, she adds, from White settlements had helped them 'avoid the physical and cultural breakdown' of the tribes around Victoria.[27] Because they had a history of meeting other peoples and were interested in other points of view, they were probably skilled in integrating new elements into their culture. The gold rush of 1858, says Usher, changed all of this. More and more Tsimshian went to Victoria and fell victim to White vices. By 1860, the Tsimshian were demoralized and had lost control over their society.

Usher's analysis is confusing, to say the least. She assumes, first of all, that the Tsimshian would only respond favourably to Duncan if they were demoralized. Hence, she identifies the year of first conversions as the year of demoralization. How does one define demoralization, and how does one judge at what point an entire group of people is demoralized? The factors she lists as agents of demoralization were not new to the Tsimshian. In fact, as argued above, they had been integral for close to seventy-five years of contact prior to Duncan's arrival. Furthermore, the numbers of converts gained by Duncan points to no mass movement away from traditional values or dissatisfaction with old ways.

Tsimshian response to Duncan may have been one of curiosity, but it was not one of acceptance. His frustration led him, in 1862, to move about fifty of his followers from Fort Simpson to Metlakatla, where he could isolate them from the temptations and influences of their non-Christian friends and relatives, and establish a model community. He also knew that this removal would free his charges from traditional obligations concerning potlatching, house-building, and feasting – a factor that no doubt appealed to some. However, most Tsimshian remained at Fort Simpson, not wishing to give up their lives to Duncan's leadership.

Metlakatla became an acceptable place to live for many more Tsimshian when a smallpox epidemic broke out shortly after Duncan's move. Throughout the summer of 1862, the disease raged through the Native camps and villages around Fort Simpson. People who knew little about Christianity flocked to Metlakatla, and appealed to Duncan to let them remain. The *Post Journal* reported: 'Mr. Duncan has at least four hundred Natives at his place; and some of them intend to build houses there and abandon this place.'[28] The devastation of the disease wreaked havoc with the social system and undermined the power of the shamans: 'Now instead of the small stream of faithful converts that had been expected at Metlakatla, Duncan was faced with several groups of panic-filled Indians who, finding no solution for their distress, were prepared to submit to the will of this missionary.'[29] People of all ages and occupational and status groups were converted.[30] While the Fort Simpson population was depleted by the disease, only five people died at Metlakatla (largely because of Duncan's vaccinations), making it an attractive alternative.

From this foundation, Duncan masterminded the establishment of a model village. Single-handedly, he managed all the activities at Metlakatla, ruling with an iron hand and forcing all the residents to conform to his decrees. Usher refers often to the fact that Duncan took 'pains to establish what had been the Indian way of dealing with situations,'[31] but, as Fisher points out, 'the point of moving to Metlakatla was to isolate converts from Indian customs, not to foster their continued existence.'[32] His village rules emphasized the departure he demanded from traditional ways:

1 To give up the *Ahlied* or Indian Devilry
2 To cease calling in conjurors when sick
3 To cease gambling
4 To cease giving away property for display
5 To cease painting their faces

These practices, central to old cultural beliefs, were replaced with rules regarding sabbath observance, religious instruction, school attendance, industry, thrift, cleanliness, and proper housing. Each element of Tsimshian life was replaced with an appropriate Victorian, Christian one.

Duncan, like other nineteenth-century British missionaries, insisted on establishing the nuclear family as an independent unit. Instead of large houses for entire lineage groups, Duncan demanded new houses, arranged in the Victorian manner, with streets running at right angles to the Coast, 'similar to labourer's cottages at home,'[33] in which each family had its own room. Traditionally, first loyalty had been to the lineage group, and members shared rights to properties, mythology, ceremonial procedures, and crests. Property now became private, with rights of succession determined by male 'heads' rather than through the man's sister's sons. Each conjugal unit was forced to fend for itself rather than existing as part of a group which worked as a unit for the benefit of all members. Lineage heads and chiefs could no longer demand absolute loyalty. With the emphasis on the nuclear family, the Tsimshian sense of cohesion, the network of people upon which one could count for aid, and the structure for social control were all replaced by the total control of the missionary.

Further social realignment occurred in the formation of ten companies of men, each with two constables and two members on the village council which, after a few years, was modified to include a chief, two Native teachers, two constables, three councillors, two musicians, and ten volunteer firemen. The purpose of the companies was 'to unite the Indians for mutual assistance, to keep each member of our community under observation (surveillance), and to give opportunity to the majority of our members to be useful to the commonwealth.'[34] The final authority, however, belonged to Duncan, and his appointment as justice of the peace in 1863 gave him the power to back his demands with the 'power of the sword' and the Royal Navy. It also gave him power to keep liquor and 'undesirables' out of Metlakatla. His Native constables guaranteed that all laws would be enforced, even going so far as to patrol the streets on Sunday to ensure 100 per cent church attendance. As Usher points out: 'Work habits, marital life, and religious beliefs of the people were all the responsibility of the police force.'[35] Fines and jail sentences were imposed for violations.

To avoid any contact with the outside world, Duncan took steps to control all the commercial dealings of his people. He asked the Hudson's Bay Company to move its store to Metlakatla, but, when the traders refused, he opened his own store and bought his own steamer to supply it. To enable the Tsimshians to have funds to buy goods from his store, he established a sawmill and several cottage industries. In 1871, he went to England to learn soap-making, spinning, weaving, and rope-making. Eventually, he taught the Tsimshian the packing and salting of fish for White markets, and, by the 1880s, the Metlakatlans had their own cannery. Duncan thus realized his goal of self-sufficiency.

Life at Fort Simpson remained more or less as it had been during Duncan's years there. Liquor and trips to Victoria continued to pose problems for both the Tsimshian and the traders. Potlatching had lost some of its impact because nearly every individual at Fort Simpson had some form of contact with Metlakatla. Lineage group co-operation suffered as a result, and, while most at Fort Simpson refused to give up old customs of status, feasting, and hereditary property, tribal obligations often remained unfulfilled because many Metlakatlans were still indebted to those at Fort Simpson and/or were not acknowledging the latter's right to consolidate their position in the traditional manner.

Despite these changes in and demands upon the social system, most Fort Simpson residents attempted to adhere to traditional cultural beliefs. There was tremendous pressure on them to abandon their old culture in favour of Western values, both indirectly from White settlers and traders, and directly from Duncan, whose main concern was to attract them to Metlakatla. The slow but steady growth of Metlakatla indicates some degree of success for Duncan's plans, but Fort Simpson always maintained a larger population. Duncan's dreams of a model utopia, including all the Coast Tsimshian, were dashed in 1873, when a small group of Fort Simpson Tsimshian were converted to Methodism in Victoria. Upon their return, they organized a public meeting, out of which was issued a call to the Methodist Church for a missionary. Neither the Tsimshian nor the missionary who was sent, Thomas Crosby, had any idea of all the factors involved in such an apparently simple request. The Tsimshian request was part of their desire for acculturation; realization of this goal proved to be a complex and difficult process, with more unforeseen conditions and problems than either the Tsimshian or Crosby could have imagined.

CHAPTER THREE

Revivalism and Civilization: The Making of a Methodist Missionary

The other party in the Tsimshian missionary relationship, Thomas Crosby, combined the Western cultural values accepted by most Anglo-Saxon missionaries with an anachronistic, revivalist brand of Methodism, similar to that prevalent in England in the middle of the eighteenth century and in North America at the end of the eighteenth and beginning of the nineteenth centuries. His cultural heritage was, in many ways, like that of Duncan and included similar notions of appropriate everyday behaviour, social relationships, and social structures. From his Methodism, he learned to place emphasis on being 'filled with the spirit' and witnessing to save 'lost souls.' By the time he arrived at Fort Simpson, he had integrated his secular and religious values into a unified package, and, for him, conversion to Christianity included the acceptance of both elements.

Crosby was born in 1840 of staunch Methodist parents, in Pickering, Yorkshire, 'within the bounds of the famous old Pickering circuit, which it is claimed has been more prolific in Methodist preachers than any other.'[1] When he was sixteen, his parents immigrated to Canada and settled in the Woodstock, Ontario area. His father's attempts at farming ended disastrously, and young Thomas was forced to go out and earn money for the family at a local tannery.[2]

Concerning his home life, Crosby later wrote: 'I was the subject of deep religious impressions. But it was not until some time later that I was savingly converted to God.'[3] During his first year at Woodstock, he was not an active church member, for, as he recalled later (in a manner typical of many evangelical missionaries), this was a period in his life during which he was possessed by a 'spirit of trifling worldliness and carelessness.'[4]

There were, however, three experiences before this time that had made lasting impressions on him. The earliest concerned a young man, George Piercy, who wished to go to China as a missionary but received no support from his family, friends, or church. Crosby wrote: 'But overcoming all difficulties, he finally did go. I shall never forget the effect it had upon my heart. I admired his piety and zeal, even though I had not as yet made definite decision for Christ, and thought that if he could leave a comfortable home and influential friends there must be an inspiring motive.'[5] The other two experiences occurred while he was crossing the Atlantic from England: sunstroke and a broken leg while on board ship gave him much time to reflect upon the meaning and course of his life. He resolved afterwards to live a Christian life, but, 'like many a sick-bed resolution, this was only made to be broken.'[6]

In 1858, a great 'Awakening' swept North America. The revival originated in the United States and was the culmination of years of evangelistic efforts. The slavery crisis, the financial crash of 1858, and growing restlessness resulting from urbanization created a climate of social and religious uncertainty, and made the warmth and promised security of evangelical revivalism attractive to many.[7] The movement spread to Canada and Europe, and it was during a revivalistic camp meeting near Woodstock that Crosby's conscience was 'aroused.' He later recalled that 'the meeting from beginning to end seemed especially for my benefit. The prayers, the testimonies, the songs were all the voice of God to my heart.'[8] After two weeks of intense inner struggle, constant prayer for forgiveness, and, finally, the conviction that his sins were 'washed away,' Crosby 'gave himself up to the Lord.' He immediately joined the Wesleyan Methodist Church and participated in the Sunday school program, the Tract Society, and the 'praying band,' a group that met for cottage prayer-meetings and visited the sick and prisoners. Eventually, he became a local preacher and spent all of his spare time reading books, 'mostly of a devotional character.'[9]

His missionary flame, first lit by Piercy, was rekindled by Rev. William 'California' Taylor, a missionary who had ministered to the gold miners of California, and whose enthusiasm kept the Awakening alive on the eastern seaboard of the United States and in eastern Canada. During 1861 and 1862, Taylor toured Canada, and the highlight of his services was a lecture about the seven years he had spent conducting revivals among the miners, merchants, and people of California. His expressive manner, with its ability to arouse sinners 'to come to the altar' and give testimony of 'pardon and peace'[10] made an indelible imprint on the mind of the impressionable young Crosby.

In 1861, Rev. Edward White, working for the Wesleyans in British Columbia, wrote several letters to the *Christian Guardian* urging young men from Ontario to come to the West Coast to serve as class leaders, local preachers, and assistants to aid Wesleyan attempts to minister to the gold miners and Natives. After having heard the messages of Taylor, Crosby needed little encouragement to go to British Columbia and do what the former had done in California. His lack of formal education and training precluded support for his efforts by the missionary society of the Wesleyan Methodist Church, but with the image of George Piercy ever in his mind, Crosby found his own means to get to British Columbia.

There were three important factors in Crosby's life that made the missionary vocation appealing. First, Crosby's family situation placed him among the lower classes of Canadian society. As Neil Gunson has noted about the nineteenth-century missionaries to the South Pacific, the majority came from the lower and lower-middle classes and saw mission work as a means of improving their station in life, a way of rising beyond their labourer's roots.[11] Second, mission propaganda, especially as used by veteran missionaries, presented romantic pictures about the missionary vocation and seemed to offer independence and freedom of action.[12] Young men, particularly those of Crosby's social, religious, and economic background, were captivated by the possibility of exchanging their tedious lower class lives for those of grand adventure, and they were stirred by the thought of undertaking dangerous and strenuous tasks for Christ. For many, the missionary vocation was the counterpoint to the lure of adventure for the hunter and explorer, inspiring 'a certain exhilaration in the fulfilment of duty and the prospect of an individual assumption of responsibility among trying conditions.'[13] Third, the nature of Crosby's Christianity, particularly its revivalistic characteristics, necessitated a life of holiness and service. The missionary vocation was seen as one of the best means to fulfil this need.

The denominational setting in which Crosby operated was the Wesleyan Methodist Church. Methodism originated in England in the late 1730s, under the guidance of John Wesley, as a movement designed to breathe life into the Anglican Church. Wesley addressed his message to the working class – the new urban, industrial, poorly educated, impoverished masses who crowded into the industrial centres to find work. He was appalled by the lifestyle, particularly the immorality and intemperance, engendered by the living conditions of these people.

Wesley's theology was an eclectic combination of various Christian traditions. From Augustine and Calvin he borrowed the notion of total depravity and the efficacy of divine grace, but he denied their views of God's eternal decrees of election and reprobation. In place of these, he substituted Pelagian and Arminian notions of free will, but not their denial of total depravity. He accepted perfectionist notions and was deeply spiritual, but he rejected religious quietism because it hindered Christian action. Furthermore, he insisted on God's absolute mercy and kindness but also on eternal punishment.[14]

The highlight of a person's life, in Wesley's Christianity, was the conversion experience – a highly emotional event that marked the point at which a person chose to reject his or her sinful life and strive for holiness. Early Methodist preachers, using a style which appealed to humble and unsophisticated people, painted lurid pictures of sin and hell and then offered God as the alternative, with the assurance that God had accepted and forgiven them and would give them eternal life.[15] Such preaching led to dramatic conversions, accompanied by such phenomena as ecstatic utterances, prostrations, and faintings. For many poor, alienated, and ill-educated working-class people, such excitement provided an attractive alternative to the tedium of everyday life. The Anglican Church, whose pastors offered little more than prudential counsel and rational belief, had little to offer these people.

Wesley's Arminian doctrines implied that all people were equal before God, regardless of wealth and status. Yet Wesley did not use his Methodism to question the inequities between the classes produced by industrialization. He was 'impressed not so much by the social evils from which the poor suffered as by the vices to which they had succumbed.'[16] Sin was not identified with the alienating consequences of industrialization and urbanization but was, rather, seen as 'individual vice and laxity' and took such forms as sensuality, blasphemy, drunkenness, and immorality. Greed, oppression, injustice, and social inequality were largely ignored because they were due to individual failings and could be cured by inner change. For Wesley, 'inward changes would produce outward effects.'[17]

Arminian equality was instead channelled into the organization established by Wesley. In each territory of his labours, he set up weekly 'class meetings' which met to hear members' testimonies and to ensure that each person followed the rules regarding such practices as sabbath observance, drinking, dancing, dress, and smoking as well as rules regarding care for fellow-members, especially the poor and prisoners. Anyone with the requisite piety could become a class leader or local preacher. Education, rank, and wealth played no part in determining leadership. Especially for poor, working-class city-dwellers, Wesley's organization provided a sense of importance and belonging missing in everyday life.

With regard to everyday life, Wesley encouraged his followers to learn to think, read, and write for themselves, and he provided inexpensive literature for their use. Furthermore, he encouraged habits of 'diligence, frugality, and cleanliness' over 'sloth, prodigality and sluttishness.'[18] Idleness was the worst of all sins; each person had to work hard, whether as servant or master, following the injunction: 'Gain all you can.'[19] The virtues demanded by Wesley fit in well with the individualistic, entrepreneurial style of commercial England, and many Methodists rapidly became wealthy. This increasing wealth, middle-class tendencies, and identification with the industrializing and urbanizing processes coexisted in an uneasy alliance with the enthusiastic, evangelical, and liberating appeal to the lower classes.[20]

Wesley's doctrines spread to the American colonies in the middle of the eighteenth century. For many colonists, the Arminian notions of equality seemed compatible with some of the prevailing democratic and egalitarian ideals espoused by a significant group within the colonies. American Methodism became staunchly 'low church,' preferring to ignore Wesley's concern for liturgy and sacraments, emphasizing instead his revivalistic enthusiasm and reducing his concern for the full range of theological concerns to a theology of conversion.[21]

In the last decade of the eighteenth century, this revivalistic brand of Methodism entered Upper Canada. The population of Upper Canada was widely scattered, and 'toil, lack of culture, [and] inadequate communication were almost universal.'[22] Most settlers were hardworking, simple, and poorly educated people who lived in constant fear of the natural forces as well as with the ever-present threat of sickness. With respect to religion, they received scant attention from the government-supported Anglican Church, whose priests made little effort to approach them.

The Methodists alleviated the settlers' chronic loneliness by establishing an itinerancy system, in which their preachers would travel from house to house, bringing the Word and news of the outside world. These preachers were often poorly educated, highly emotional men, who, because of their humble origins and temperament, could appreciate the qualities necessary for frontier life and, travelling in spite of a negligible transportation system, shared the hardships of the settler. They were 'skillful exhibitionists; they put on a good show because they knew it got results.'[23] Their emotional appeals aroused a state of religious excitement, particularly at the large camp meetings which emerged in 1803. Vivid pictures have been painted of the mass hysteria, faintings, and dramatic conversions which occurred after highly impassioned, bordering on irrational, appeals by these preachers.[24] They saw a whole generation who stood near 'the gates of hell' and, following the lead of Wesley, saw people as creatures born in sin, needing spiritual regeneration. Sin and hell were presented in the darkest terms, calculated to arouse in the hearers a sharp sense of guilt that would lead to impassioned appeals for God's grace. Egerton Ryerson saw the essence of revivals as two-fold: 'The *suddenness* of conversion and the extraordinary circumstances connected with them.' Conversions were indeed dramatic, accompanied with 'physical agitations and prostrations.'[25] Natural phenomena and personal incidents were seen as signs of God's direct and personal intervention in the lives of each person.

The North American Methodists thus adopted an 'enthusiastic' rendering of Arminian Wesleyanism. Furthermore, they duplicated Wesley's system of class meetings, complete with testimonies and scrutiny of fellow-members' lives. As in Britain, Methodist leadership was chosen on the basis of piety, and daily life was regulated by the same prohibitions on forms of behaviour such as drinking, gambling, dancing, and swearing. For the lonely settlers, the Methodist services, with their lively hymnody, camp meetings, and class meetings, provided intimacy and fellowship. Fellowship was more important than theological training or Biblical scholarship; after all, the Bible was the literal work of God. The realities of sin and judgment, in a hostile environment, were the most pressing matters and could be overcome by a vivid conversion experience. All aspects of the Methodist presentation and organization were geared to disturb the conscience of the hearers and lead them to a decision for Christ.

Canadian Methodism in the early years of the nineteenth century was merely an extension of the Methodist Episcopal Church of the United States. The colonial government's fear of anything American in the years following the war of 1812[26] and the coming of the conservative British Wesleyan Methodists shortly afterwards led to dramatic changes within Canadian Methodist circles, both in organization and in spirituality.[27] Organizationally, the Canadians severed all connections with the 'enthusiastic' American Methodists in 1828 and joined the more sedate British Wesleyans in 1833 to form the Wesleyan Methodist Church of Canada.

The change in religiosity was just as noteworthy: 'By 1825, the Methodist community in Upper Canada had become closely integrated with the life of the province in personnel and in outlook and had matured sufficiently to realize that its responsibilities might include more than the simple preaching of the gospel in its Wesleyan form.'[28] By 1830, the camp meeting had become formal and arranged, lacking the religious outbursts of earlier years. In fact, this was generally true of all facets of church life; stereotypical actions and clichés prevailed as the church moved into the second generation. Perhaps, as H. Richard Niebuhr has pointed out, the first generation had won its convictions while the second saw them as a heritage.[29] Preachers were now required to have formal education as well as zeal.

Many of these changes occurred as the frontier style of life disappeared.[30] The increase of settled areas, the greater wealth of the population, and their acquisition of higher culture and learning negated the factors which had been responsible for the highly charged revivalistic gospel. The itinerant preacher was replaced by a paid, stationed pastor; a professional clergy meant moderation, and sermons became polished speeches rather than rambling outbursts. By 1840, professional evangelists had replaced the revivalists.

The union with the British Wesleyans also made a dramatic impact upon Canadian Methodism. After Wesley's death in 1791, the British Wesleyan Church had become the church of the Industrial Revolution's new and wealthy bourgeoisie – conservative and politically quietest in outlook. These Methodists formed the bulwark of British Toryism in the first decades of the nineteenth century. When they came to Canada, the Canadian Methodists, who up to this time had been identified with Reformers such as Mackenzie, reversed their political allegiances and disassociated themselves from all Reform policies. They also moved from a voluntarist position and accepted limited state aid for their churches. The Wesleyan Methodist Church gradually became identified with the politically conservative and the emerging commercial and industrial sectors of the colony.[31] It became the church of the successful, especially in the towns.

Indeed the world was changing for the citizens of Upper Canada: 'Commercial and industrial expansion, the growth of cities, the spread of education, and the improvement of the means of communication with the outside world led to a deterioration among the population generally of evangelical religious values and to a strengthening of worldly attitudes and outlook.'[32] The world contained such new marvels as the telegraph, newspapers, railways, steam power, and world travel as well as such ideologies as materialism and nationalism. By mid-century there was a general conviction that the age was one of 'improvement' in religion, science, and literature, and that the most glorious days of the human race, when the human mind would be free of the fetters of earlier ages, lay ahead. It was the era of growth and progress in a land blessed by God with bountiful natural resources.[33] Methodist literature, particularly the *Christian Guardian* and Ryerson's *Journal of Education*, lavished praise on the new science and technology of the day, promoting industrialization, along with Christian morality, as the route to a better world.

In terms of church life, this confidence of the 1850s and 1860s was reflected in the construction of palatial churches, complete with parsonages. Theological training and formal education for pastors was seen as essential if the church was to keep abreast with the new developments and demands of the age. Camp meetings were now held at resort areas and were more like holidays with religious services than long, drawn-out revivals. While the church was still predominantly evangelical, gone were the emotional extremes and excesses of earlier years. Most members were humble, sincere Christians, prosperous and well-to-do, and politically conservative. Older members complained that religious zeal had departed from Methodism, and the constant loss of members to 'holiness' groups indicated that there probably was a significant change in spirituality in Methodist functions.[34]

Canadian Methodists were, however, not too far removed from their roots to be unmoved by certain expressions of religious fervour. The Awakening of 1858 and missionary tours by such colourful figures as William Taylor elicited enthusiastic responses and would continue to do so for many more years to come, even though the dominant trend in Methodism was away from such expressions.[35] But, for everyday life, Arminian evangelical enthusiasm was inappropriate, and as Bernard Semmel has noted about English Methodism in a somewhat different context, enthusiasm was channelled into missionary work: 'In this way the doctrines of Evangelical Arminianism, and the evangelistic Enthusiasm of the converted might continue to be fulfilled with safety, even while Methodism, in pursuit of respectability, contributed to the national mission.'[36] Methodist missionaries, both in early nineteenth-century England and mid-nineteenth-century Canada, were frequently replicas of the old itinerant, revivalistic preachers, and they aspired to create revivals with dramatic conversions and signs of the Holy Spirit.[37] They still looked for and found the direct hand of God in everyday experience, even as the world was becoming more manipulated, analyzed, and secularized. Mission work was an outlet for people of their temperament – people not usually found to be suitable for the home ministry.

These missionaries were, moreover, more than mere revivalists. Their aim was also 'the furthering of the world mission of the English [and Canadian] middle-class.' As Melville Horne stated: 'Foreign missions will have the same influence on religion, as foreign commerce has upon agriculture and manufactures.'[38] What religion had effected at home would be reproduced in the mission field. The spread of religious and commercial, technological values belonged together.

Thomas Crosby, whose beliefs and values were similar to primitive, frontier-type Methodism, accepted this particular combination of Christianity and Western civilization. He heartily endorsed the emerging commercial and industrial way of life. The simple evangelical gospel was accompanied with all the latest 'benefits' introduced by technology, and, indeed, the latter became an integral part of the Christian message. The Canadian social structure and cultural values, complete with Christian religious symbols, formed an integrated whole in Crosby's eyes and was presented to the Native people as such.

In 1862, Crosby arrived in British Columbia. After a particularly long voyage by sea, Crosby attended his first Methodist service in Victoria. He wrote: 'I was like a bird let out of a cage and entered with joy into the spirit of the meeting. It was afterwards asked by some of the brethren: 'Who was that strange boy in home-spun clothes who had the audacity to disturb the quiet of the church by his "Amen," "Hallelujah," and "Praise the Lord"?'[39] His zeal was rewarded in March 1863, when he was appointed to assist Cornelius Bryant at Nanaimo and teach at the Native school despite his lack of formal education or, as typical of virtually all nineteenth-century missionaries, training to deal with non-Western cultures.

Crosby's first response to the Native people among whom he lived was one of both fascination and repugnance.[40] He was convinced of the need to learn Native languages to be an effective teacher, and he spent much time at Native feasts and councils, listening to the chiefs and orators recount hunting tales, war deeds, and other stories of courage. He recalled 'how the old orators would rise with the enthusiasm of the occasion and seem to make the ground tremble under their feet as they rejoicingly told of the names and deeds of their fathers, to fire the ambitions of the young princes and young men of rank.'[41] He was impressed by the absence of swear words in Native languages as well as their hospitality, generosity, and natural musical ability. Native people, he said, claimed to get their music from the 'wind in the trees, from the waves on the seashore, from the rippling stream, from the mountain-side, from the birds, and from the wild animals.'[42]

But admiration for some elements of Native society did not lead to a general tolerance of basic Native practices. He wrote: 'I cannot have anything to do with the old way, the dance, the potlatch, etc., it is all bad.'[43] For Crosby, 'everything of heathenism, is of the devil.'[44] The potlatch was the worst vice of all. Its conspicuous consumption and distribution of goods and food was totally reprehensible to a frugal, hard-working, Victorian Canadian. Native hospitality and generosity could not outweigh a basic 'heathen' orientation. Crosby noted that miners, for example, could buy Native women because 'heathenism crushes out a mother's love and turns the heart to stone and changes the father into a foul indifferent fiend.'[45]

Because Native society was so corrupt, it had to be abolished and replaced by something similar to Canadian society. Crosby felt unable to teach school adequately if the children did not attend regularly, wash themselves with soap, and wear 'proper' clothing. He noted that the parents and old people were often indifferent to the school and 'showed very little appreciation, often indeed taking the children away with the most silly excuses.'[46] Christianity was not enough: 'We felt that the education of the people would not be complete unless they were taught habits of order and industry. Their old houses and their surroundings were wretchedly filthy and disorderly, and little calculated to help them in their efforts to rise.'[47] Shortly after he began work at Nanaimo, new, one-family houses were built on individual lots, adorned with picket fences and gardens, and organized in a straight line. The school and mission houses were known as 'Christian Street,' and the houses on the beach were known as 'Heathen Street.' The Natives were encouraged to take up agriculture and farming as part of a program to teach them 'the gospel of self-help.'[48]

Crosby's approach to Native society was established in his early years of work for the Wesleyans. His particular style of presenting the gospel developed after he left the school at Nanaimo. In 1866, Crosby became an itinerant preacher, accompanying Rev. Edward White on a circuit which covered the east coast of Vancouver Island, from Comox to Victoria, including stops at Chemainus, Salt Spring Island, Cowichan, and Saanich, as well as journeys up the Fraser River. In 1868, his spirited preaching at Chilliwack led to a six-week revival, with nightly meetings and four Sunday services. He recalled: 'The spirit of God was present in mighty awakening power, and the whole neighbourhood was moved.'[49] During this revival a young Native convert, David Sallosalton, preached, and, because of his preaching, 'the whole congregation rushed forward to the rude altar of prayer, and then scores of people with one voice sent up their cries and petitions to heaven for salvation.' Many of these were Native people, and the Whites, reported Crosby, were amazed and tearful 'at seeing so many of the red men anxious for pardon.'[50] Some of the most 'hardened sinners' were 'awakened' and converted to the gospel. A class was established at Chilliwack and, in 1869, Crosby was appointed to work there. In June 1868, a camp meeting was held at Maple Bay, and, in September of the following year, one was held at Chilliwack. The old Methodist revival technique and the outdoor, open camp meeting style became Crosby's favourite means of presenting the gospel.

In 1871, Crosby was ordained and appointed as missionary to all the Native people of British Columbia.[51] In 1872, he made a foray into the Interior. In seventeen days, he travelled 482 miles; held twenty-seven services for both the English and the Native people; preached in court houses, hotel bars, log cabins, and outdoors; and visited the Lytton, Kamloops, and Nicola people before returning to Chilliwack. During the winter of 1873-4, Crosby was given a furlough to Ontario and went on a tour with Rev. Egerton Ryerson Young, a missionary stationed in Manitoba, 'and the twain marched as conquering heroes of the cross.'[52] He also met and married Emma J. Douse from Hamilton. While in Ontario, he received notification of his appointment as missionary to Fort Simpson.

The three factors leading Crosby to take up mission work remained operative during his entire life as a missionary. The desire to rise socially, the lure of adventure, and the nature of his Christianity continued to act as stimuli inspiring Crosby to work in these remote areas to convert the many 'heathens.'

First, Crosby had risen above his tanner's background and family circumstances. As one of the oldest of fourteen children, in a poor family, Crosby's obligations would have placed severe limitations on his ability to rise socially. By 1871, however, he was an ordained Methodist preacher, having acquired this position without the requisite training – a training which he probably would have been unable to receive had he remained in Ontario. His appointment to Fort Simpson gave him independence and responsibility and, over the years, he became the most famous Methodist missionary in British Columbia, if not all of Canada.

Second, the lure of adventure and danger remained a powerful stimulus in Crosby's life. During his years as an itinerant preacher on the circuit along Vancouver Island, he travelled by canoe and faced innumerable dangers in the ever unpredictable waters of Georgia Strait. He wrote:

> In journeying to and fro I travelled over two thousand miles a year in all kinds of weather, braving the dangers of stormy seas and the eddies and swift currents of treacherous rivers; and enduring the discomforts of the wild open life in a new country. In it I see the good hand of God saving me from manifold danger.[53]

In one particular year, he crossed Georgia Strait four times, paddling from Nanaimo to Yale and back twice. He compared himself to the miner and adventurer: 'In time one becomes used to such toils and difficulties, and, after all, they were only the common, every-day experience of the miner or the frontiersman of those early days.'[54] In later years, he recalled with delight the consternation of a friend who once remarked, 'Crosby, you will kill yourself; you are a strange fellow.'[55] This attraction to adventure was not quenched when he went to Fort Simpson, where much of the surrounding area was largely unexplored and undeveloped by Europeans. He spent a great deal of his time organizing and covering a circuit which involved thousands of miles of canoe travel per year. He always seemed happiest being outdoors and 'roughing it.'

Finally, and most important, the nature of his Christianity, which saw gratitude for conversion as being best expressed by 'winning souls' for Christ, was constantly reinforced by his exposure to those who were culturally and religiously so different from him. For missionaries such as Crosby, life before conversion and without Christ was heinous, even if the sins were no greater than laziness, impure thoughts, and occasional swearing. Demonstrative exhibitions during conversion experiences were, for Crosby, visible signs of the reality of that experience. It was especially critical to bring this saving knowledge, with all of its manifestations, to those who had never been exposed to the 'fruits' of the gospel and whose heathenism made them totally degraded. The urgency to spread the gospel to the countless 'unsaved,' and the necessity for observing visible signs confirming conversion, remained with Crosby all of his life.

When Crosby arrived at Fort Simpson in June of 1874, therefore, his missionary approach had been clearly established. He knew what he wanted to do and how to go about accomplishing it. The Tsimshian had to become replicas of Western Europeans in how they lived and worshipped. Conversion was, of course, the primary requisite, but, for Crosby, the only suitable context for conversion was that of the complete Western way of life. In effect, he was attempting to build a new cultural framework for the Tsimshian, complete with a new social structure and religious symbols. The interaction was, therefore, a cultural confrontation and not merely a religious one. Rather, both the religious and secular aspects of this relationship were part of, and illustrated clearly, the nature of the wider cultural interaction. The fact that the Tsimshian themselves wanted to participate in Western culture at this time gave every indication that the mission would be successful.

CHAPTER FOUR

Tsimshian Acculturation: 'Religious' Life

One of the key factors leading to the Tsimshian call for a missionary at Fort Simpson was the fact that they had been in contact with European civilization for almost one hundred years. They had witnessed European technology, lifestyle, economic practices, and religion, and had observed the dramatic changes accomplished by Duncan at Metlakatla. An important reason for choosing Methodism was its revivalistic style of worship – a style which reminded them of their own winter ceremonies and religious practices. The course of events concerning 'religion' and worship is, thus, an integral part of, and reflects, the way in which the wider cultural interaction between the Tsimshian and Crosby developed.

Of central importance to the relationship was the fact that it was the Tsimshian rather than the Methodists who had been responsible for Crosby coming to Fort Simpson. During the first years of the Methodist presence at Fort Simpson, this fact was virtually ignored, while the Methodists and Anglicans, particularly William Duncan, hotly debated their respective 'rights' to this territory. The Methodist decision to come to Fort Simpson was a response to Tsimshian wishes and not an arbitrary decision to invade an Anglican, in this case Duncan's, territory.

The key instruments in this call to the Methodists were Alfred and Kate Dudoward, a Tsimshian couple, both of whom had European fathers and had descended from chiefly families. Alfred's mother was from the house of Legaic, and, through his marriage to Kate, he ascended to the leadership of the Gitands tribe.[1] He was brought up and educated at Metlakatla and for a time was a servant in Duncan's household. Kate, on the other hand, went to Victoria as a young girl and was educated at an Anglican school, there achieving proficiency in reading, writing, and speaking English. In the late 1860s, she returned to Fort Simpson and established a school to teach the Tsimshian European skills. A short time later she married Alfred.

At Fort Simpson, Kate remained faithful to her Anglican upbringing while Alfred attempted to return to traditional Tsimshian customs and ways of life. Duncan reported that he 'broke away from my influence ... While our Native teachers were busy at Fort Simpson enforcing gospel truth, he was engrossed in heathenish customs and took the lead of a cannibal party there.'[2] In 1871, Duncan, in his role as justice of the peace, fined Alfred twenty blankets for selling liquor and obstructing justice.[3] Duncan promised to return the blankets if Alfred behaved properly for a specified period of time. The blankets, however, were never returned, and Duncan claimed that Alfred even tried to bribe the village council to return them to him.

In the spring of 1873, Alfred and Kate went to Victoria to visit the former's mother, who had recently been converted to Methodism at one of a series of revival meetings being held there, and he, too, was converted. Later that summer, Alfred, Kate, and a number of other Fort Simpson Tsimshian attended the annual camp meeting in Chilliwack. Upon their return to Fort Simpson, they continued to meet as a small group of Methodists. Kate resumed teaching at her school, this time supplied with books and materials by some of the Methodists in Victoria.

Duncan responded to this Methodist presence by intensifying his labours at Fort Simpson and sending Native preachers there each weekend to minister to those Tsimshian sympathetic to his work. In the winter of 1873, at Duncan's invitation, 200 Fort Simpson Tsimshian came to Metlakatla to celebrate Christmas. William Collison, Duncan's assistant at the time, reported that the work at Fort Simpson was showing promising results: 'The good seed which has been sown from time to time is now springing up and bearing fruit.' Many of the Fort Simpson people, he added, had promised 'that henceforth they would walk in God's ways and abandon their heathen practices ... Many of them have intimated their intention of coming to Metlakatla to live.'[4] In his annual report, Duncan informed the Church Missionary Society that the tide of heathenism was turning: 'This is the first season that the heathen customs at Fort Simpson have been generally disregarded, and hence we thought it well to encourage Christian customs in their place.'[5] According to Duncan, the gospel was steadily replacing Native heathenism and drunkenness; sabbath observance, law and order, and a 'general thirst for religious instruction' were becoming the norm.[6]

In the meantime, the Methodists made a series of moves to establish a permanent mission at Fort Simpson. In response to Native calls for a missionary, William Pollard, chairman of the British Columbia district (Toronto Conference) of the Wesleyan Methodist Church, went to Fort Simpson early in 1874 to determine whether or not one should be sent. He bypassed Metlakatla, thereby neglecting to consult Duncan, and met with several delegations of Fort Simpson Natives. By 27 February 1874, he had baptized 125 children and 14 adults. His final conclusion was that the area needed a full-time missionary, and Crosby, in Ontario at the time, was appointed. In the meantime, Charles M. Tate was appointed to act as interim missionary. He arrived on 4 April 1874 and immediately held daily services and established a Sunday school and two day schools with 300 pupils, both adults and children.

Duncan reacted immediately to Pollard's visit by stepping up the services at Fort Simpson and even making a rare appearance there himself. What upset him most was that Pollard had not even consulted him about the need for a new missionary in this area. Duncan felt that there were so many other areas on the Northwest Coast that needed a missionary more, and that, in any case, the trend at Fort Simpson was towards Christianity. He also believed that there had been some collusion between his 'old enemies' among the Native people and the Hudson's Bay Company with respect to persuading the Methodists to come.[7] In March of that year he wrote that he had heard reports from Native people claiming that Pollard had promised them wealth in the form of oxen, steamers, and sawmills, and, furthermore, that the Methodists had no objections to the Tsimshian mixing with Whites – a prohibition central to Duncan's policies.[8] Over the next year, Duncan and Pollard exchanged several bitter accusations. Duncan accused the Methodists of indiscriminate baptisms, peculiar worship practices, slander against Metlakatla, and the incitement of a spirit of rivalry and division.[9] Pollard, in turn, accused Duncan of neglecting Fort Simpson, instilling the fear of man rather than God through his magistrate's office, inducing the Fort Simpson Natives to leave their ancestral homes for Metlakatla, and depriving Metlakatla Natives of legal rights because he, Duncan, owned the land.[10] In addition to this bickering between Duncan and Pollard, hard feelings existed between Tsimshian followers of the Church Missionary Society and the Methodist Tsimshian at Fort Simpson. Duncan claimed that people were still leaving Fort Simpson to come to Metlakatla.[11] In a more conciliatory tone, Collison, in August, stated that it was sad to see the promising work at Fort Simpson disrupted but that there was cause for rejoicing because the gospel was being presented: 'If Christ is preached therein do we rejoice.'[12]

The confrontation between the Church Missionary Society and the Wesleyan Methodists centred around their respective claims to the territory. When Pollard accused him of neglecting Fort Simpson, Duncan countered with the assertion that he had never abandoned it. The issue became even more heated when Rev. J.B. Good charged the Methodists with usurping an Anglican field. Pollard simply replied that the Fort Simpson residents wanted the Methodists, and, more pointedly, the Church Missionary Society was also interfering with Methodist mission fields in other parts of the province.[13] It almost seemed as if the Tsimshian were merely pawns to be played off and divided between the churches as the latter saw fit.

While the missionaries argued about their rights, they neglected to mention that the Tsimshian themselves had been instrumental in persuading the Methodists to come to Fort Simpson. Matthew Johnston, sixty years later, recalled that Duncan had not neglected Fort Simpson after he had left for Metlakatla but had remained active there, and, as a result, trading patterns and practices had been altered and liquor abuses curbed. Kate Dudoward, also in 1934, stated that she had simply changed churches while at Victoria and had gone back to Fort Simpson with books and Bibles, encouraged by the Methodists to continue her work. Meanwhile, Duncan's laymen, she added, maintained regular services each Sunday. Both Matthew Johnston and Kate Dudoward note that, at this time, there was a feeling at Fort Simpson that there should be a change, and a public meeting was called to discuss the matter. However, no final decision was made. Somehow there was an understanding that, on the following Sunday, the group that rang the first bell would be the choice of the people. A lesser chief, Hahis, took matters into his own hands and rang Kate's school bell. The people flocked to her school building where Kate conducted the first Methodist service. From this meeting, a call was issued for a Methodist missionary. Pollard's visit, they concluded, gave the Dudowards the authority to carry on Methodist services, and, shortly afterwards, a missionary was sent.[14] It is revealing that the debate between the missionaries centred on their rights to the area rather than on Tsimshian wishes, when the records and sources clearly indicate that the Methodists had more followers at Fort Simpson than had Duncan.[15] Shortly after Crosby's arrival, at the beginning of July, the Methodists had Fort Simpson to themselves.

Duncan encouraged his followers not to bear grudges against those who preached the same gospel. Nevertheless, Duncan himself took considerable time to accept Crosby. In November of 1874, as magistrate of the district, Duncan sent Crosby a terse letter in which he wrote that he had been notified that Crosby had opened old Native graves and moved the corpses to a cemetery near Fort Simpson. One particular Native had not been notified of this move. Furthermore, the sanction of the provincial government had to be obtained before Native graves could even be visited. He added: 'As I cannot therefore suppose you would wilfully do an unlawful act I deem it right before issuing a summons to acquaint you with the charge and await your explanation in this.'[16] Crosby replied that he had thought that all parties involved had been present when he made the move, and that he certainly would not have acted contrary to their wishes. He promised to make reparation to any aggrieved party. Duncan advised Crosby that even if Native people agreed with this action, the matter was still a violation of provincial law. He demanded that Crosby obtain the signatures of all parties involved so that the provincial government would be aware of the situation and thus end the problem.

Duncan was also dismayed by Crosby's methods of presenting the gospel. In the winter of 1874-5, some Anglican Natives from Kincolith worshipped at Fort Simpson, and, during prayer 'all prayed *aloud* at once – Mr. Crosby in English. The others – some in Tsimshian, some in Nishkahh ... each prayed whatever came into his mind at the time, and thus they turned the sacred office of prayer into a ... Babel of tongues.'[17] Duncan also accused Crosby of baptizing children of pagan parents from Kincolith, an Anglican territory. When Duncan asked him why he had not consulted him first, Crosby replied that he did not see any reason to do so as Duncan himself had been at Fort Simpson several times since Crosby arrived and had never visited him.[18]

In 1877, Duncan was contemplating leaving Metlakatla because he refused to bow to pressure from the Anglican church to accept ordination.[19] While he was in Victoria in the fall of that year, a revival broke out at Metlakatla, encouraged by his assistant, Rev. A.J. Hall, who had delivered a sermon on Joel 2:28-9, concerning the outpouring of God's spirit.[20] The Metlakatla Tsimshian loved it, and, in a short time, there were reports of angels, conversations with the Holy Spirit, exorcisms, dreams, ecstasies, and other similar experiences.[21] Apparently, Crosby came to Metlakatla and encouraged these activities. When Duncan heard that Crosby thanked God for the revival, he was sure that he had a good idea of the kind of things happening at Metlakatla. According to Duncan, 'he [Crosby] was a well-meaning and able man, but very impulsive and emotional. A veritable shouter of shouters, who had managed to get some of the Indians into what almost amounted to a religious frenzy.'[22] As Usher notes, Duncan's appeal, as an evangelical, was to the heart – but 'through the mind and understanding' rather than the emotions.[23] Duncan returned to Metlakatla to restore order, more determined than ever to preserve his work of twenty years.

In time, Duncan and Crosby managed to set aside differences and establish friendly relations. By 1880, there is evidence of a general exchange of goods and information.[24] In 1881, Duncan and his council invited their fellow-Christians from Port Simpson[25] to celebrate the Christmas season with them. While the church officially declined the invitation, upwards of 400 did attend the subsequent New Year's day celebrations.[26] Indeed, as Duncan experienced greater difficulties with the parent society, and particularly with Bishop William Ridley, over the ordination issue,[27] the Methodists became his allies. In 1882, he recalled how the coming of the Methodists had initially brought division to the area, but that the gospel message had produced a loving atmosphere.[28] Duncan and Crosby co-operated on the Native land issue, and, when it became apparent that Duncan was about to leave Canada because of his problems with the Anglicans and the federal government, Crosby wrote: 'What a shame to our government that one thousand good industrious people are driven out of our country by them from their home and the land of their fathers.'[29] When Duncan left, the Methodists supplied their mission boat to move the people and their possessions from Old Metlakatla to New Metlakatla in Alaska.

Although Duncan gradually accepted Crosby, Crosby's style of presenting the gospel did not change. The revival method, which had so upset Duncan in 1877, remained, for Crosby, the ideal. The emotional revival setting, with its attendant manifestations, was confirmation of the presence of the Holy Spirit and of the reality of the conversion experience. Everything that Crosby attempted to accomplish at Port Simpson was of secondary importance to the primary task of having the Tsimshian renounce sin, in a highly dramatic conversion, and demonstrate, as a consequence, a zeal for saving other souls.

The Tsimshian had initially been attracted to Methodism at the revival style meetings at Victoria and Chilliwack. This style of gospel presentation was continued by Tate during his few months at Port Simpson. At his first meeting with the Tsimshian, he reported that there was spontaneous singing of such songs as 'Come Every Soul by Sin Oppressed,' followed by prayer. He began praying, but soon everyone was praying. He reported:

I thought this hubub could not be in order; but when I opened my eyes, and looked into the tear-streaming faces of those hundreds of anxious souls, I cried from the depth of my soul, 'Hallelujah! The Lord can hear a thousand prayers at one time just as well as one,' and the reception service was turned into a very Pentecost.[30]

When Crosby arrived later that summer the revival was still in progress. With his powerful voice and dominating presence, accompanied with lively and rhythmic Methodist hymns, Crosby and his gospel appealed to the song-loving and dramatic Tsimshian. In a short time he had persuaded them to contribute generously to the building of a new church and, by 1876, a pretentious frame church dominated the Port Simpson landscape.

As a Methodist, Crosby instituted the whole array of Methodist religious functions. As soon as possible he established class meetings to provide a setting in which the members could express their new-found faith. In addition to a number of Sunday worship services, there was Sunday school for adults and children. During the week there were also special services and prayer meetings. Whenever revivals broke out, services were held daily. Crosby also established an itinerancy system which followed the Port Simpson Tsimshian to their spring and summer fishing and berrying grounds as well as embracing the Native villages along the Nass and Skeena, down the coast to Bella Bella, and across the water to the Queen Charlotte Islands. For ten years he covered this circuit by canoe, spending much time away from home and usually accompanied by Native assistants. He generally spent two or three days at each place, dramatically informing Native people of their sin [due to the Fall] and of their need for Christ to save them. Invariably, the villagers were led to desire their own missionary and, by 1897, there were nearly a dozen permanent missions on the Northwest Coast.

All of this work, however, only assumed importance when Native people made dramatic renunciations of their old ways and maintained an enthusiastic and lively response to God following conversion. Such emotional highs were difficult to maintain. In 1875, Pollard observed: 'The change is so decided, and the improvement is so visible to all who come in contact with them, that it is the subject of remark all along the coast.'[31] Less than a year later, Crosby reported that the Tsimshian were not attending church as well as they were at first: 'There was a falling off, which was very painful to us.'[32] From this time on, until the day Crosby left Port Simpson, his letters repeated time after time the need for 'blessed revivals' and 'outpourings of the Spirit.'[33] Crosby lived for revivals, as if they were confirmation of the effectiveness of his work, and, indeed, of his own faith. Problems in secular areas involved much of Crosby's time and energy, and, as we will see, were often a source of extreme frustration. During one particularly trying time with the government, he wrote Ebenezer Robson: 'But I do not like to refer to these matters.'[34] A living, demonstrative faith, with visible signs of the Holy Spirit's presence, was more important than anything else. Indeed, revivals often meant the neglect, for weeks at a time, of every activity but worship.

In 1877, a revival occurred after the church had been damaged during a November storm and the Tsimshian had given liberally to have it repaired. It was a typical frontier Methodist revival, due 'in a great measure to the fact that the poor had made such sacrifice for God's house, for in some cases they had given all their earthly goods.'[35] Describing the scene, Crosby wrote:

> Hundreds of people crowded into the Church where many of them fell on their faces on the floor, crying to God for mercy. For some time that scene continued and many were blessed ... On leaving the church ... they nearly all fell down on the ground as if they were under a strange spell and began pleading earnestly for God to have mercy on them.[36]

Forty adults were baptized in December of that year and several new classes of baptismal candidates were formed.

There was another revival early in 1881 when an old man died and in a few weeks, 'nearly every old man and woman were [sic] in attendance in class and prayer meetings, and it resulted in our receiving 60 or 70 by baptism,' some of whom had been 'on trial for years.'[37] In November of 1882, after returning from a trip to the many coastal preaching places, Crosby found the people in the midst of another revival. He wrote:

> This is what we have been praying for. Many of the most indifferent had been clearly converted. We had prayer-meetings every morning at 7 o'clock, and at 2 P.M. some earnest ones would gather in the street to sing, then proceed to some house for a meeting. And at half-past six there would be service in the school-house, when the people would come singing up the road like a Salvation Army.[38]

At such events the 'hardened sinners' would be prayed for, exhorted to beg for forgiveness, and then sung to with such songs as 'Come Every Soul by Sin Oppressed, there's Mercy with the Lord.' Frequently the responses would be dramatic and the penitent would respond with phrases such as: 'come back, Lord, come back; please don't leave me, come back, Lord Jesus, and forgive me.'[39]

By the mid-1880s, while church services and prayer meetings were well-attended, class meeting attendance began to decline and revivals were virtually non-existent. Fellow missionary, and Crosby's assistant, A.E. Green, reported in 1890 that

> we have been very much grieved by some who years ago were leaders in the work of God, but who, becoming cold, would lead the people back to the old customs that they gave up, as bad, when they first received the gospel. Many have been drawn away during the past three or four years to take part in the old heathen practices.[40]

The missionaries complained that the Tsimshian were too busy with other things to pay proper attention to spiritual matters. Their celebrations, particularly weddings, had become, according to the missionaries, ostentatious, wasteful displays, reminiscent of the potlatch which they had officially given up. The desire for revivals grew more earnest each year, and in the winter of 1890-1, when a revival seemed near at hand, 'Alas! some who were prominent made missteps and fell ... Then as the festive times came on, the people entered them with far too much zest for their own good ... In many cases the old heathen pride showed itself.'[41] But as a true nineteenth-century evangelical missionary, who believed in God's personal intervention in the lives of people, Crosby reported: 'God has been speaking in loud tones to the sinning. Some in the prime of life have been taken away.'[42] For Crosby there was always solace in the fact that God did not let sin go unpunished and, in his writings, he was always sure to illustrate graphically examples of people who had sinned, usually by violating the sabbath, and had met misfortune of some sort.

The last revival at Port Simpson, during Crosby's tenure, occurred at the end of 1892, ten years after the previous one. Whereas each spring the Tsimshian would scatter all over the province to find work in fishing, lumbering, or in hopfields, that year a smallpox scare kept them at home, where they fished and hunted in more or less the aboriginal manner. Smallpox was avoided, and, under the direction of the missionary, thanksgiving was channelled into an event where the 'Spirit came down in power and crowds came forward to the penitent bench.'[43] From 30 October until February, services were held daily. Every day 'backsliders' were returning to the Church, and very few residents were left 'unsaved.' The meetings were extremely lively, as Salvation Army songs were sung, and often five or six people would speak at one time, filling the air with 'Amens' and 'Hallelujahs.' The meetings usually lasted until after midnight. Crosby reported: 'Of course, our meetings are very lively; but the power of God is so manifest that everything is kept within bounds ... All have got a fresh baptism of love and power.'[44] The revival was capped by a five-week missionary tour up the Skeena River by Crosby and his Native enthusiasts during October and November of 1893. Despite cold weather and the fact that nearly all participants had influenza, they continued the tour, singing songs such as 'There is a Happy Land' and 'We'll Work Till Jesus Comes,' and carrying banners with such inscriptions as 'Come to Jesus' and 'Seek Ye the Lord.'[45]

In 1894, Crosby reported that the revival was spent and that some members had 'fallen.' This situation was not unique, as church membership records, particularly between revivals, record the frustration of the missionaries at the consistent failure of the Tsimshian to maintain missionary expectations of the Christian life. The Port Simpson Register is full of examples of members who shifted from full membership to 'on trial' and then back again to full membership over the twenty-three years of Crosby's residency. A particularly illustrative example is that of Alfred Dudoward. Although Dudoward had been largely responsible for calling the Methodists, and had acted as a class leader and local preacher during Crosby's first years at Port Simpson, he was placed on trial in 1880 and even dropped from the list in 1887. He was either on trial or a full member most other years, until he joined the Salvation Army in 1895.[46] From 1887 to 1896 in particular, there was a constant juggling of leadership positions in the church (local preachers, class leaders, leaders, and exhorters) as well as a constant movement of people between 'on trial' and full membership status. There were few who managed consistently to remain in good standing and maintain their leadership positions year after year.[47]

This constant falling in and out of grace with Crosby underscores the growing tension previously noted in reference to the lack of revivals and the recurrence of old forms of behaviour. The problem seemed to be a power struggle between the wishes of the people and the will of the missionary. Bradley Lockner and Archibald Greenaway largely attribute Crosby's difficulties to his failure to go beyond primary evangelization.[48] While this certainly is an important factor, the problem was deeper. As early as 1878, Crosby admitted that he was often absent from Port Simpson, but he felt that this would '[beget] a general missionary spirit among the people.'[49] Crosby was often away from home for weeks at a time, visiting the missions or establishing new ones. His love of adventure and desire to spread the Word sent him on trips that covered hundreds of miles, entailed considerable risk, and involved numerous preaching encounters with Native people. In 1880, he reported that he had travelled 2,700 miles by canoe and had been 'caught in storms when there seemed the greatest danger.'[50] In 1882, he toured Ontario and returned to Port Simpson in July; by November, he had again travelled 1,000 miles. A two-week trip up the Skeena, in September of 1887, covered 460 miles, and, within a few days of his return, he was off again to Bella Bella. Such reports dominate his writings and his letters to Ontario, no doubt with the aim of stirring his readers with tales of adventure so that they would, financially and prayerfully, support God's work in British Columbia. While stationed at Port Simpson, he acquired the services of a mission boat, *Glad Tidings*, launched on 29 November 1884, and he averaged 9,000 miles a year on it.

The problem of Crosby's mobility was complicated by the fact that the Tsimshian themselves were absent from Port Simpson for long periods of time, usually scattering during January or February, travelling all over the province to find work and not returning till the fall. The soil at Port Simpson was not fertile enough for farming, and markets were too distant for industry to be economical. Crosby and his cohorts constantly complained about how this unsettled condition hindered continuous religious work as well as how it placed their parishioners in 'surroundings less conducive to growth in the Divine life than at home.'[51] As a result, many of them returned home 'cold' and as 'backsliders.' This nomadic existence was, of course, not new for the Tsimshian. The nature of their mobility, however, did change after Crosby's arrival, and traditional subsistence activities were replaced with wage labour. The new lifestyle demanded by Crosby necessitated a cash supply, as traditional sources were unable to provide the money for the new styles of housing, community living, clothing, food, and entertainment. The more the Tsimshian became dependent on a wage economy, the further they had to go for work and the longer they had to stay away from home.

Thus both parties contributed to the instability of the relationship. But Crosby's absences were more crucial, as he had come to Port Simpson with the purpose of changing certain conditions of Native life. Furthermore, the Tsimshian had also wanted Crosby to lead them, and Albert Nelson, in 1885, expressed a widespread feeling when he complained that 'Mr. Crosby does not stay at home; he goes to visit other places, and when he is gone there is no one to direct us.'[52] As we will see later, these were critical years for the Tsimshian in terms of the land question, and Crosby's frequent absences, when he was expected to be a leader, were not taken lightly.

In addition, aboriginal Tsimshian religious expressions, particularly as represented in the winter ceremonials and potlatches, were totally vetoed by the missionaries. As at Nanaimo, Crosby displayed absolutely no tolerance for Native customs, especially religious ones. He did attempt to replace some of them with the lively Methodist hymnody, Christmas celebrations, and the Methodist New Year's Watch Meeting as well as by creating some secular organizations such as a volunteer rifle corps, volunteer firefighting units, and a brass band – each organization resplendent with badges and uniforms. But as Rev. R.B. Cuyler, missionary at Bella Bella, wrote, 'The old system of feasting and dancing gave something for their sensual natures; the new system denied these and . . . did not satisfy the soul's desires.'[53] Barnett's rather crude representation of Tsimshian religion perhaps explains why revival gospel appealed to the Tsimshian: 'The central feature of the Tsimshian cultural belief and ritual was the demonstration of bodily possession by a variety of mythological spirits which caused the possessed individual to act in rapturous and often inhuman fashion.'[54] The fact that revivals were predominantly winter phenomena suggests that they were substitutes for the old winter ceremonial complex, which, to the consternation of the missionaries, resurfaced more strongly when there were no revivals. Crosby saw revivals as antidotes to 'pagan, heathen' rituals and celebrations and, as noted above, complaints about the lack of revivals coincided with the despair which Crosby felt about the persistence of traditional religious practices.

By the end of the 1880s, the Tsimshian dissatisfaction with the situation was recognized and two moves were made to alleviate the tension. Crosby's travelling was seen as a problem, for, as he said himself, 'It is impossible to do justice to this mission and be most of the time away from it.'[55] During the years 1889 and 1890, Crosby was appointed to be the full-time missionary on board *Glad Tidings*, while Dennis Jennings (1889) and A.E. Green (1890) ran the Port Simpson mission.

The second move was more significant. Recognizing the need for Native religious expression and trying to stem the tide of dissatisfaction and restlessness growing among the Tsimshian, the missionaries permitted the formation of the Band of Christian Workers whose primary purpose was evangelism. In Crosby's early years, Native enthusiasm for evangelization had been channelled into allowing them to accompany him on his missionary tours. But by

1884, Crosby found it difficult to acquire this aid: 'I had to paddle my own canoe with but one man with me [as] it is now more difficult than it was years ago to get a crew.'[56] The Tsimshian no longer seemed to be content with taking a back seat to the missionary. As Thomas Wright explained in 1885 to Alexander Sutherland, General Secretary of the Methodist Missionary Society, the Tsimshian, and not the Whites, had first brought the gospel to Port Simpson, and, therefore, they wanted the church to train Native teachers. He pointed out that 'Alfred Dudoward went to Victoria, and he and his wife came back bringing the Word of God in their hands.' The Tsimshian, he added, brought the gospel to all the tribes in the surrounding area: 'They have been trying to follow God from the first. I tell you this because the white men say they were the first; but it was the Tsimshian. They are a strong people.'[57] Others complained that Crosby's absences prevented instruction in Christian living and since they themselves were incapable of reading or explaining the Bible, they felt unsure about the holiness of their lifestyle.

It is therefore understandable that the enthusiasm which the missionaries were unable to channel into revivals was expressed in the Band of Christian Workers. At its formation, Jennings reported that

> by earnest prayer ... their hearts were first prepared for this work. Men were found going into the Church, cold and dark, and there, alone with their God, they would pour out their souls in earnest prayer to Him that seeth in secret, and they were rewarded openly. They waited not in vain for the descent of the Holy Spirit, for his presence was manifested in their looks, their words and in their increased zeal.[58]

The Band members engaged in open-air services with street preaching punctuated by prayers and shouts; lively music accompanied by drums, horns, and tambourines; banners and flags with various slogans and texts; and elaborate parades and showy uniforms. Green reported that the Band engaged in Sunday services outside of the regular Sunday worship services, and, during the winter, held services during the week as well.[59] The Band had its own president and secretary, and frequently accompanied Crosby on his missionary tours. Initially the Tsimshian were pleased with this increase in control over their religious expression, but Crosby made no moves to begin a training program for Native religious leaders. Gradually, the Tsimshian came to realize that permission to form this band had been granted only because the missionaries did not see it as a threat to their power. That they realized this very quickly is indicated by their relationship to the missionaries after 1891.

The initial missionary response to this group was one of approval, as it provided a religious outlet for the Tsimshian not available in the church. The missionaries were generally patronizing to the group, as is evidenced by the certificates issued by the Ministerial Session in 1889 to the Band of Christian Workers' members: 'Go ye into all the world and preach the gospel. This is to certify that _____ is a member of the Band of Christian Workers in connection with the Methodist Church at _____ Mission. He that winneth souls is wise.'[60] They saw the Band as a harmless safety valve through which religious enthusiasm could be displayed while church services remained orderly. Often, when the rest of the Church at Port Simpson seemed dead, the Band convinced the missionaries that their work was still bearing fruit. Paradoxically, during the years that the missionaries were frustrated with the lack of revivals, the renewal of old customs, and the need to place long-time members back on trial, they were happy about the work of the Band, an organization which embraced most of the young and many of the old people of the church.

Yet the root causes for the Band's existence did not disappear. In secular and religious matters, the Port Simpson Tsimshian, in the 1890s, were determined to exercise more control over their destiny. This fact is graphically illustrated by the course followed by the Band after the first few years of its existence. In the spring of 1892, the Band requested permission to use its instruments in church, and the missionaries cautiously permitted it 'whenever it becomes expedient' but only after consulting with, and obtaining the approval of, the missionary.[61] The previous winter the Band members had also expressed a desire to build their own worship building, but the village council, with Crosby as its head adviser, had turned down this request, and the missionaries advised the Band to abide by this decision. The Band also addressed the Ministerial Session, announcing that they had extra money and wished to send out Native evangelists. The missionaries 'resolved, that while this [sic] good yet this should be done in cooperation with the minister and the Chairman of the District and should not be collected and spent without consulting them.'[62] Clearly, the issue at stake between the two parties was one of power.

The Band persisted in its demands for increased participation in worship services. Contrary to the wishes of the missionaries, by the end of 1893, the Band chapter at Port Simpson had its own building, but, as Crosby noted, all of the members still attended the regular church services.[63] The Ministerial Session of 1894, responding to the growing assertiveness of the Band, stated: 'We reaffirm the resolution of last year in regard to the use of musical instruments and recommend to each missionary the organization of Band of Christian Workers to be *controlled* by the missionary in charge.'[64] Nevertheless, in the summer of that year, Band members Henry Tate, Sam Bennett, Robert Tate, and Peter Jones went out with Captain William Oliver of *Glad Tidings* to preach to other tribes of Native people. The Band advised caution before undertaking such a mission, while Crosby, interestingly, endorsed their action. The Tsimshian felt that what was significant about this action was that 'this is the first time that we ... have started out by ourselves to carry the gospel.'[65] At the end of 1894, Crosby admitted that for the past three years the Band had not been under the power of the church because the members wanted power to control their own affairs while still belonging to the Methodist Church.[66]

The issue of control was further complicated by the intrusion of the Salvation Army. Sometime in 1894, a group of Port Simpson Band of Christian Workers' members joined the Salvation Army while they were in Victoria and started separate services when they came back to Port Simpson. When the Salvation Army prepared to move into the northern missions, Crosby and Ridley, the Church Missionary Society missionary, took Ensign Edgecome of the Salvation Army on a tour of the area to show him where help was needed. Nevertheless, he settled on Port Simpson and Port Essington as two bases from which to operate. As R. Geddes Large notes: 'There was, of course, a reason for this, as the Army did not have the personnel to carry out missionary work on a large scale, and relied in most cases on dissenting Native leaders of the established churches and their disgruntled followers.'[67] In many ways, the Salvation Army paralleled the Band in its expressive emotional worship, rousing music, street preaching, and colourful apparel. Tsimshian desire for control of their own worship was probably as responsible for attracting members to the Salvation Army as it had been for attracting members to the Band seven or eight years previously. According to William Beynon, intense rivalry within the Band for leadership positions prompted many to go to the Salvation Army.[68] Towards the end of the decade, the Band was virtually independent of the Methodist Church. In response to this situation, the missionaries introduced the Epworth League as a society in which Methodist Christians could channel their enthusiasm. The Band of Christian Workers, the Salvation Army, and the Epworth League competed vigorously for members and were responsible for many hard feelings among the villagers of Port Simpson. This complicated situation prompted one of Crosby's successors to remark, 'I enjoyed missionary work till I came here.'⁶⁹ Eventually, the Methodist Church regained its lost members and the Band of Christian Workers, though in existence until 1942, occupied a less important place in the community. The Dudowards, for example, left the Methodist Church in 1895, but in 1897, Ebenezer Robson had reopened communication with them and Kate was again employed as an interpreter.

The establishment of Salvation Army missions at Port Simpson and Port Essington violated one of the basic unwritten rules of Northwest Coast mission work: that of non-interference in the missions of another church. Generally, the Church Missionary Society and the Methodist Church of Canada avoided trespassing on each other's territory and divided the northern coast between them. Crosby had little trouble dealing with such Anglicans as Duncan, Tomlinson, Collison, or McCullagh. His only conflicts with the Church Missionary Society were with Duncan's nemesis, Bishop William Ridley. Over the years there were isolated charges by each party concerning usurpation of territory that had not traditionally been theirs: Skidegate in 1882, and the Skeena River area in 1880-1 and again in 1885-6.⁷⁰ Nevertheless, harmony was the goal in missions, as is evidenced by Ridley's and Crosby's alliance against Salvation Army intrusion in 1895.

There was, nevertheless, a deep rift between Crosby and Ridley. As we will see later, much of Crosby's dislike of Ridley stemmed from the apparent ease with which the Anglicans received the ear of the two levels of government while the Methodists were ignored. Ridley's dislike of Crosby, on the other hand, arose largely because of Crosby's friendship with Duncan,⁷¹ and because of their very different practical approaches to mission work. Ridley disdained Crosby's emphasis on revivalism. According to Ridley, while Methodists always boasted about their 'Pentecostal successes,' their people frequently lapsed into heathenism because their Christianity was only nominal.⁷² Their problem, he said, was that 'they preached, preached and preached and left their people as ignorant and ... as bad morally as ever.'⁷³ He recalled: 'I remember when their missionary there reported wonderful "Pentecostal revivals." Within a brief space about five hundred conversions were supposed to have taken place. The days were not long enough for prayer and praise and the nights were turned into days. Instead of envy I felt dread.'⁷⁴ Ridley emphasized strict discipline and lengthy instruction. Between 1885 and 1898, Ridley translated the Gospels, the Epistles, the *Book of Common Prayer*, and the Liturgy and Ritual of the Anglican Church into Tsimshian. Duncan and Crosby, while performing all their services in Tsimshian, left the Bible and other theological works in English, requiring parishioners to learn English to acquire more insight into their religion.

Rev. S.S. Osterhout concurred with Ridley's analysis of Crosby's work. In 1898, he reported that he was teaching a course in doctrine: 'I am afraid that in the past they have been unduly urged to preach, preach, preach without having been first taught what they should preach, hence the fanaticism so present.'[75] This statement would seem to support Lockner's and Greenaway's position that Crosby's falling out with the Tsimshian and the rise of the Band of Christian Workers and Salvation Army was due to his inability to go beyond primary evangelization. Indeed, the deeper faith and knowledge demanded once the conversion experience had occurred was not readily available to the Tsimshian. Such arguments, however, look at the Native response to missionaries from the viewpoint of missionary leadership.

It is significant to note that the Church Missionary Society, including Bishop Ridley, responded to the same Tsimshian restlessness experienced by Crosby and Green by allowing the establishment of a Church Army at each of their Northwest Coast missions. The Church Army was similar in organization and function to the Band of Christian Workers and, later, to the Salvation Army. Collison claimed that it had been organized to avoid allowing Native enthusiasm to get out of hand.[76] But the important thing to note is that even in missions where instruction dominated, the Native people of the Northwest Coast were demanding control of their own means of worship. The missionaries, Anglican and Methodist, had to accommodate their wishes. To understand why the Band of Christian Workers and Church Army developed, it is imperative to look first at Native reasons for their formation rather than at missionary policy or leadership. As we will see in the next chapter, the move towards self-determination in religion was part of a movement by the Northwest Coast people, and particularly those at Port Simpson, to establish an identity in the changing world of the late nineteenth century. It is crucial, despite missionary disclaimers, to see that the Tsimshian remained dedicated *Native* Christians, who took their religion seriously and lived it, as one would expect from them, expressively and emotionally. By the 1890s, they wanted to set up and have more control over their lives. The missionaries, whose outlook was essentially paternalistic, saw this attitude as an attack on their work and as evidence of unchristian motives. They failed to recognize Native people as partners in the 'work of God,' seeing them instead as children who needed guidance to attain the maturity of their White

Christian brothers and sisters. By the 1890s, many Port Simpson Natives no longer tolerated such an outlook.

Crosby's difficulties with Native people were compounded by his frustrations with his parent society, the Missionary Society of the Methodist Church of Canada. During the 1895-7 conflict with the Salvation Army, Crosby informed Ebenezer Robson of his desire to have a full-time person to work at Port Simpson and to help deal with the difficulties.[77] Throughout his years at Port Simpson, Crosby's letters echoed with the desire to have additional workers on the Northwest Coast. As early as 1876, Crosby complained that appeals for missionaries were going unanswered. Repeatedly that year, he asked for missionaries on the Nass and Skeena and for Alaska. The field, he said, 'is ripe for harvest, I fear that if something is not done speedily, these opportunities may pass forever.'[78] He felt that he could not go back to these 'poor' people and say that the church was praying for them but could not send missionaries: 'Will the Church be true to her trust?' he asked.[79] He could not conceive of the church not providing people for the work: 'And shall these souls be left to perish? My soul says no; I know you will say no; and trust the missionary committee and the whole Church will say No! No!!'[80] All over the Coast, he reported, the 'Macedonian call'[81] for missionaries was reaching him.

Not even his stirring accounts in the missionary and church periodicals of adventurous journeys and dramatic conversions could attract young people. In the early 1890s, the situation became desperate as far as Crosby was concerned: 'It is too bad that the West Coast should be left and the people are passing away and we have with the Boat the means of reaching them with the gospel if we had the men.'[82] He was short of people in every area of the district and was worried that the Methodist hold on the Coast would weaken. When, from 1895-7, the mission at Bella Bella remained vacant because the missionary board was unable to attract any workers, he sent his own daughter there for a year. The strain and frustrations of the years were beginning to tell. In June of 1895, reflecting on the shortage of workers, he wrote to George Raley: 'It is too hard, too hard, the Lord help us.'[83] By this time he was in his mid-fifties and he no longer had the stamina or desire to cover the distances he had in his younger years. In the early years, the shortage of workers had led him to cover every area himself, but, as he noted about his 1894 trip up the Skeena (when he pointed out that his absence of four years in this area had considerably lessened the influence of his ministry),[84] he no longer felt up to regularly undertaking such demanding journeys.

The kind of person that Crosby felt was suitable for missions had to be 'a man of faith, full of fire, and music – a man ready for all work, and a first-class teacher.'[85] The editor of the *Missionary Outlook* put it this way: the qualified person would have to be a missionary, a teacher, an architect, a carpenter, a builder, and a doctor; someone who could 'paddle his own canoe' and be 'able and willing to turn his hand to anything'; not salary conscious but full of 'holy enthusiasm,' with 'gifts of head and hand and heart.'[86] While such appeals had an immense attraction for people (such as Crosby) whose social, educational, and economic backgrounds made missionary work appear as an attractive alternative to their present situation, the conditions among the Methodists in the 1880s and 1890s did not make Native missions attractive.

The world of Ontario had changed dramatically since Crosby's departure in 1862. New inventions and techniques introduced by capitalism had increased productivity in industry and agriculture, opened up new means of communication, and generally improved the standard of life. There was a widespread feeling that the world was becoming a better place in which to live. The Methodists had many of the new capitalist class (the nouveau riche), among their number,[87] and Methodist periodicals reflected their readership's wide interest by dealing with such subjects as science, world's fairs, exotic places, classical Greece and Rome,[88] and drama and literature.

These material and cultural improvements, however, were also accompanied with such doctrines as materialism, nationalism, socialism, and evolutionism – doctrines involving ideas which seemed to remove God from direct involvement in human affairs.[89] The question of higher criticism dominated Methodist circles in the 1890s, with opinions ranging from those who believed in the literal truth of the Bible to those who held that it was influenced and conditioned by human beings.[90] As well, there was an uneasy recognition that Methodism had become the church of the wealthy and had lost its traditional appeal to the poor and to the lower classes. Social agencies were established in the 1880s to minister to the poor,[91] and by the mid-1890s there was a growing movement within the church that linked, theoretically and theologically, socialism and Christianity.[92]

In such an environment, to many, missions seemed less important than many of the bigger questions of the day. In many ways, Crosby was a quaint anachronism and his tours in Ontario (1874, 1882, and 1889) did revive memories of the 'heroic age of Methodism.' The *Christian Guardian* reported that 'his appeals ring out like a clarion blast rousing the zeal and quickening the liberality of the people.'[93] The editors of the *Missionary Outlook*, who constantly decried the lack of Methodist generosity to mission work, noted that Crosby's tours brought in record amounts of money.[94] But within a year of his 1882 tour, for example, the editorials of this magazine complained that interest in missions had again declined in favour of other entertainments. Indeed, while the church increased its membership by two and a half times between 1874 and 1894 and doubled the value of its church property between 1883 and 1894, the mission fund only increased by 70 per cent.[95] Interest in missions began to decline as other contemporary issues demanded more time and energy.

Native missions seemed especially hard hit by this lack of interest. The *Home and School* reported that 'in these days when increased missionary zeal in Japan, India, and China engrosses so much attention, we are liable to overlook the comparatively obscure, but more arduous, labours of our missionaries among the Indian tribes of the North West and British Columbia.'[96] Tales about Native heathenism and idiosyncrasies had lost their ability to fascinate and disturb, and Native people were increasingly seen as a persistent problem that would not disappear. After many years of contact with a 'superior civilization,' they still had not become Westernized. Missionary zeal, by the end of the nineteenth century, 'was mostly stimulated by distance and exotic customs.'[97]

In addition to manpower shortages, Crosby was constantly frustrated by the lack of funds provided by the Missionary Society. As early as 1876, he reported that he was fixing up an old house for a school rather than building a new schoolhouse 'as the Missionary Committee are not able to assist us.'[98] The problem of financing became especially acute during the late 1880s and the 1890s. In 1887, Crosby accused the mission board of favouritism towards foreign missions.[99] In 1889, Alexander Sutherland sent Crosby a sharply worded letter concerning his budget submissions for that year. A request for $500 for 'one to be sent' and one of $500 for a boy's institute were rejected out of hand because, although the British Columbia Conference had approved these items, the Board of Missions had not. He felt that the 'establishment of a precedent of this kind would be very dangerous' because the annual conferences 'cannot establish a new Native mission without the concurrence of the Board.'[100] A short time later Crosby was notified that 'the recommended grants of the Port Simpson district are beyond what the necessities of the work require, and if allowed would be out of proportion to the amounts allowed in other parts of the world.'[101] In that same letter, Crosby was also advised that his expenses for his 1889 leave would not be paid by the Board, as his last furlough had been seven years ago and the rules required a period of ten years between furloughs. He wrote: 'But there is more involved in this matter than a mere money grant, it involves the question of the right of any brother to leave his work whenever it suits him, and to spend months abroad, then send his bill for travelling expenses to the Committee for payment.'[102] The question of funding was thus more than a question of the availability of money; the issue between Crosby and the Society was really that of control. Crosby felt that he was the one best suited to determine the needs and costs of the missions because he lived in the area. The Mission Board, on the other hand, controlled the finances and was determined to get a good return for the money invested. It was reluctant to give in to every request of a missionary, who, if he had had a free hand, would have placed missionaries in every Native village on the Northwest Coast. Just as *they* were accountable to the Methodist Church for the sound use of mission funds, Crosby had to be held responsible to *them* for the proper and efficient management of his district. For Crosby, the frustration was intense, as it meant that he had to do more work himself and that fewer Native people would be 'saved.' One can only imagine his reaction when Sutherland told him, in 1897, to make his absences from Port Simpson 'few and far between.'[103]

Throughout the 1890s, Crosby was advised to forget about any extension of his work. In 1894, Crosby had to inform his missionaries of a 5 per cent cut in their salaries. In 1895, Sutherland wrote Crosby that there would be a 'discount on the salaries, and nearly all grants for buildings had to be refused.'[104] The salaries were further discounted the following year and all 'minor' items, such as buildings and supplies, were eliminated from the budget.

Crosby's difficulties and frustrations with the Tsimshian and the Methodist Church (and other denominations) as well as the problems of his methodology seem, on the surface, to support the notion that the decline of the mission was due to the failings and inabilities of the missionary and his parent society. However, the example of the Band of Christian Workers clearly demonstrates that the Port Simpson Tsimshian wanted to throw off the yoke of paternalism. The issue at stake was much wider than the mere acceptance or rejection of Christianity or of the missionary. The interaction between missionary and Native was a confrontation between two worldviews – not merely an attempt to effect religious change. As noted above, religion is but one element reflecting underlying cultural values – a symbolic way of rendering basic beliefs and values satisfying. The movement towards self-determination and self-expression in matters of worship and religious expression was thus but one aspect of a move that had its parallel in virtually every facet of Tsimshian life. Both the secular and religious facets of the relationship between the missionary and the Tsimshian were parts of a deeper cultural interaction.

— change to Canadian ways did not let them be an accepted part of the society with political determination. This fight was a Native fight, not one induced by

CHAPTER FIVE

Tsimshian Acculturation: 'Secular' Life

the missionaries. The inability for Natives to gain power was not missionaries fault per say but the general attitude towards Natives in the 19thC.

The Tsimshian move towards self-determination in the area of worship was paralleled by a similar development in secular, everyday affairs, matters of lifestyle, social structure, and economic concerns. After the 1874 decision to call a missionary, most Port Simpson Natives desired to replace much of their traditional Tsimshian culture with that of the Europeans. In the early years, eagerly following their missionary, Crosby, they seemed to be making rapid progress towards their goal, and there seemed to be an almost iconoclastic attitude towards anything Tsimshian – despite the fact that some Tsimshian ways of living and thinking persisted. They made virtually no effort to resist Crosby's program to dismantle their culture. Gradually, however, they came to the realization that they were not becoming 'full Canadian' citizens, and, as in church life, they demanded more control over this process. Although it is true that Crosby's methods were most effective in establishing new missions, the Tsimshian move towards self-determination was largely due to circumstances beyond his control.

In the nineteenth century there was tremendous optimism about the increasing state of 'civilization' among an ever greater number of people. This view had a profound influence upon missionaries sent to minister to 'backward heathens,' as they linked this advancing tide of civilization and progress to the spread of Christian truth.[1] Moral and practical education was seen as the vital ingredient in encouraging the spread of civilization. Missionaries such as Crosby, therefore, made it a priority to establish schools on their missions and to design curricula which not only taught the basics, such as reading, writing, and arithmetic, but also appropriate attitudes towards work, recreation, home life, and social relationships. Crosby believed that Christianity could not flourish unless it was set in a proper cultural environment, and, furthermore, that only Christianity could establish that proper setting. Thus, the setting (Victorian) and Christianity were perceived as a unit.

Both the Tsimshian at Port Simpson and Crosby believed that the coming of the gospel would make a dramatic impact on the lifestyle and social patterns of the former. The Tsimshian had the example of Metlakatla, where Duncan had established a radical Victorian alternative to their traditional culture. Despite the Port Simpson rejection of Duncan, many features of his model village doubtless lay behind the Native call for a Methodist missionary; events during the first years of the mission confirm this desire. Shortly after her conversion, Kate Dudoward was encouraged by the Methodists to continue her school so that Tsimshian children could become a 'great people': 'Then when the young people grow up they can learn trades, and professions – become carpenters, blacksmiths, doctors, lawyers, preachers, and be a blessing to themselves and society; and the women will become good and respectable mothers of decent families, and respected by their white sisters.'[2] The Methodists offered a model and the Tsimshian accepted – not necessarily interpreting the model in the same manner.

When Tate established the mission, church services and school classes were instituted simultaneously. Crosby continued this emphasis on education because, as he noted, 'Our way to a heathen tribe was often through the school.'[3] Paralleling the goal of church work, the ultimate aim of the school was to introduce a totally different way of life – a way comparable to that of any White village in Canada. It was as crucial to teach Native people the gospel truths about the fall, sin, and atonement as it was to show them 'how to work for a living.'[4] By eliminating heathen practices and teaching the children new ways, the missionaries hoped to raise a new generation – a generation which would be a credit to British Columbia society.

Unfortunately, from the missionary point of view, schooling was an immensely frustrating process. School records indicate that few Tsimshian received an education beyond the elementary level. Attendance was always poor; the daily average attendance was always well below half the number of students enrolled. Pollard noted that because the 'parents have not the least idea of the necessity of an education, you must first educate the parents to allow their children to attend school.'[5] The migratory habits of the people and the need to travel for life's basic necessities such as fish, meat, and berries, he added, worked against a large daily average attendance, as almost all of the families were away from Port Simpson for extended periods of time. Later, when the Tsimshian had adopted many of the trappings of White society and had become more involved in a wage economy, their new way of life continued to necessitate lengthy absences from home. The day schools, during all of Crosby's years, never did attain a high degree of stability.

Crosby found it as difficult to attract and keep teachers as he found it to get missionaries. Between 1882-94, there was virtually an annual change of teachers.[6] In fact, during the winter of 1891-2, the teaching of the school was divided between Crosby, his wife Emma, and Matron Hart of the Crosby Girls' Home. In 1893, the mission staff recognized that this constant change of teachers led to restlessness among the Native people and hindered continuity in education.[7] Charles M. Richards, appointed in 1894, was the first teacher to remain at the day school for an extended period of time, providing a more stable educational setting.

Because the migratory lifestyle of the Tsimshian limited their school attendance, the missionaries decided that a boarding-home approach would be appropriate, as it would give the children both the time and the setting in which to learn 'civilized' manners and lifestyles as well as remove them from the 'negative' influences of their parents. The first such institution was the Crosby Girls' Home, opened by Emma Crosby in 1879, in response to the need to rescue young girls from the vices of liquor and prostitution associated with travel to the south. Many of them were destitute orphans, generally of mixed-blood, for whom the mission house was a means to escape the evils of travelling. The Home also received girls who were brought there by relatives who felt incapable of preventing their girls from falling victim to the evils of White contact. The aim of the Home was to train the girls in what were considered to be the proper feminine graces: cooking, sewing, embroidery, washing, hygiene, mothering, and serving. When they reached the marrying age, they would be good Christian wives to their husbands and would raise honourable Christian families in decent Christian homes.

The discipline in the Home was rigid, for as Kate Hendry, matron of the Girls' Home in the early 1880s, stated, the care of the girls required 'a great deal of Grace, Patience and determination they are so obstinate and disobedient. Yet I wonder I never get angry with them for I have to punish them quite often it being the only way you can make them mind.'[8] The matrons of the Home had to constantly battle a spirit of restlessness and discontent and had to be on guard against the ever-present threat of 'heathen' friends enticing the girls away. On one occasion, two girls ran away from the heavy work load and were apprehended and brought back by the village constables.

Kate Hendry reported that 'they were locked up in our work room nearly a week where I had talked to and prayed with my two prisoners every day.'[9] Very often the girls did not perceive their duties in the way envisioned by the directors of the Home. Emma Crosby reported that the girls were eager learners as far as civilization was concerned, but that sometimes they did not keep their priorities straight – 'they want to play the organ before they know how to make bread.'[10] The girls stayed at the Home until they were married, at which time a new girl would be admitted. The missionaries were generally pleased with the effects of the training, as many of the girls later conformed to the lifestyle taught by the Home.

In the late 1880s, the continued mobility of families prompted the missionaries to expand the Girls' Home to include boarders and also to build a Boys' Institute. The lifestyle of the parents was not conducive to fostering proper habits. The boarding-homes would provide the training and discipline which the parents were unable to give, for, according to Crosby, the parents, 'though kind and indulgent to their children, are not capable of teaching and controlling them properly.'[11] In 1890, the Boys' Institute was opened, and the boys were taught to cut wood, cook food, do dishes, and sweep the house. The aim was to develop 'good men, if properly trained ... but who may turn out the very worst if left to evil influences.'[12] In 1892, a new Girls' Home was built to include boarders as well as orphans and needy girls.

Another service provided by the mission was medical aid. Initially, the missionaries served as doctors, working especially hard to give smallpox innoculations. Over the years, however, the missionaries in the area were not able to provide all the medical services necessary to curb the high mortality rate among the Tsimshian. In fact, Crosby lost three of his own children. But again the Missionary Society was unwilling to pay for a medical missionary.[13] In 1889, Crosby took matters into his own hands and appointed Dr. A.E. Bolton to take care of all medical matters. For Crosby, the power of medicine was crucial in defeating the all-powerful hold of the shaman. In medicine, he felt, he had 'one of the most effective agencies in spreading the glorious Gospel of the blessed God.'[14]

In 1892, a hospital, funded by the Methodist Missionary Society and the federal and provincial governments, was established at Port Simpson, and a few years later another one was built at Port Essington. In addition, Dr. Bolton travelled extensively to Native villages, administering medicine and aid to those who needed it. He became a justice of the peace in the mid-1890s as well as being a preacher, so no doubt his power was not lightly regarded.

Providing education and medical services was, however, only part of the wider goal of mission work. The whole living environment had to be conducive to the kind of life promoted by education and Christianity. As Crosby wrote later: 'The Missionary who cannot teach the Native or heathen how to build his home or cultivate his land, or is too lazy to do it, is not a practical or successful Missionary. How can a man teach religion and not teach industry, cleanliness and thrift of all kinds, for the Bible is full of such lessons?'[15] The first priority was to change the living quarters of the people. Crosby was appalled that several families resided in one building, where members of both sexes and of all ages slept, ate, and lived together: 'With such lessons of human wickedness ever before their eyes, is it any wonder that the children, left under such conditions, were morally corrupt?'[16] Crosby felt that there was no better way to illustrate Christian living than by a

> good and well-ordered Christian home. If he is walking 'in his steps' the teacher will naturally illustrate by the fields, the sower, the harvest, the birds, the fish and by everything around us, and should be able and willing to show how to build a nice little home ... Indeed, this is the only way to win the savage from his lazy habits, sin and misery ... get them out of the wretched squalor and dirt of their old lodges and sweat houses into better homes.[17]

The new homes advocated by Crosby were three- or four-room houses, one for each individual family unit. By 1877, there were thirty new houses; by 1881, there were ninety; and, by the end of the 1880s, all the old houses had been torn down along with their totem markers. The houses were laid out in orderly streets, lit by street lamps, and were decorated with picket fences, gardens, and shrubs, in a manner, reported Indian Superintendent I.W. Powell in 1879, 'which would not do discredit to any civilized town in more populous places.'[18] Powell noted that totem markers had virtually disappeared and that personal decorations and Native ornaments now appeared only on the old. In that same year, Crosby reported that in the space of five or six years the Tsimshian had given up the 'grossest heathenism,' including such practices as dancing, conjuring, drinking, or gambling and now made up one of the most orderly communities in Canada. All kept the sabbath and were industrious.[19]

To effect such changes, Crosby felt it necessary to inculcate new attitudes towards work and property. In his first year he reported that the Native people needed to be dealt with patiently because of the poor attitudes inherited from their old way of life: 'One gets sick, another lazy, a third wishes to get a wife, another to go fishing. There is always some trouble.'[20] They did not seem to have the drive necessary to 'get ahead' and 'rise' socially, to engage in economic activities in a manner which would bring them surplus, 'cash' wealth. Furthermore, while their respect for nature was admirable, it prevented the exploitation of resources needed to become wealthy. To Crosby, it was necessary to teach the Tsimshian 'to help themselves' and to become self-reliant, as this was the practical side of the gospel. A few miles away, at Georgetown, a sawmill was established and run by a Mr. Williscroft in order to provide lumber for the new houses. Crosby was convinced that if Native people saw the need for new houses and built them at their own expense, proper habits of thrift and industry would be formed. The people also contributed generously to the new church, and school children were encouraged to pay for their own books and supplies. In addition to these measures, Crosby instituted an annual Port Simpson Industrial Fair in 1875, to which the Tsimshian could bring and display products made over the previous year. Prizes were awarded for the best entries in needlework, knitting, beadwork, patchwork, woodwork, carving, model-building, drawing, and vegetables and foods because Crosby believed that, like children, Native people would be motivated to work harder if they were rewarded. The show was discontinued after a few years because Crosby could not get the governments to contribute money and prizes.

The Tsimshian view of property, according to Crosby, also worked against individual initiative. Nearly every material item, including the houses, belonged to the clan. In fact, this group acted as a unit in all matters and individuals acted only as members of a group. Crosby noted that public assent was required for any and every activity and that the acknowledgment of that assent occurred in the potlatch – a wasteful, time-consuming event in which individuals gave away all their wealth, leaving no savings for future necessities or investments.[21] Only when men perceived the need to work hard for themselves so that they could save money and provide houses for their individual family unit, that is, acquire private property, could any real progress towards civilization occur. Crosby was aware that this move to individual houses would cause a state of confusion because old debts would remain unpaid. As he noted, giving up the old way 'left the property very unequally divided; some are now very poor, while others are better off.'[22] However, he believed that the end result was more important than the temporary imbalance of obligations.

To ensure an orderly development of the new village and to enforce the new laws required by the new style of living, Crosby established a village council. He felt that the Tsimshian way was lawless, and, as there was no justice of the peace, some mechanism had to be used to regulate both the development of the village and the laws for everyday living. In a shrewd move, he suggested that the most powerful individuals of the community be appointed to the council, people such as the 'conjurors,' 'gamblers,' and 'man-eaters,' that is, shamans, members of the dancing societies, and other leaders in the festivals and celebrations. He correctly calculated that the conjurors would make laws against gambling, for example, and that, in response, the gamblers would make laws against conjuring.[23] The council regulated such village matters as sanitation, road-work, street-lighting, and other public works and also passed laws on sabbath observance, feasting, liquor consumption, domestic disputes, and even marriages between Christians. Watchmen were appointed to enforce these laws and a committee of the council made regular searches through houses for such items as gambling pins and medicine paraphernalia. Infractions were punished with fines, which were used for public works. Crosby was the chairman of the council, and, in effect, it merely approved his policies. Crosby stated that the Tsimshians governed themselves 'under the direction of their missionary; and no more peaceful or quiet community could be found.'[24]

In the early years, the Tsimshian eagerly followed Crosby's tutelage. They clearly wanted what Crosby offered them. In October of 1878, the chiefs and leaders of Port Simpson wrote the Superintendent-General of Indian Affairs David Mills, requesting some aid in the form of garden implements, nails, window sashes, and other such items to complete the construction of their new homes and streets. They wrote:

> You will be pleased to learn that although it is only four years since we gave up the old ways of our fathers, that there is a great change in our village. We have now no heathen feasting nor dancing, conjuring, gambling and drinking which were so degrading and ruinous to us as a people. And that in the place of these we have a Church and school, which we enjoy much. Also our houses and village are undergoing a great change.[25]

The fact that church membership rolls (including full members and those on trial) never included much more than one half of the Native people at Port Simpson while, at the same time, all residents adopted the new standards and abandoned their old houses in a short period of time indicates a strong desire on their part to become part of Canadian society.

Unfortunately, from the missionary viewpoint anyway, adoption of White religion and civilization was not a simple matter of rejecting one way and accepting another. Old habits of living and patterns of thought could not be obliterated by a simple desire for their disappearance. Certain practices that had been used for centuries were so engrained in the Tsimshian way of life that they continued despite many outward changes. For Crosby, Native acceptance of both Christianity and civilization entailed certain norms and forms of behaviour which, he assumed, belonged together by their very nature. The Tsimshian did not always make the same connection and, therefore, saw no contradiction between many of the new ways and some of the old ways. Indeed, some of Crosby's demands seemed so abhorrent and unnatural that they could not accept them.

This tension is reflected in the establishment of the village council in 1880. For Crosby, the council was a community council responsible for policing, sabbath observance, sanitation, building, entertainment, and schooling. Alongside of this new institution, the traditional Tsimshian council of clan chiefs, which had been responsible for the regulation of such village activities as potlatches, initiations, name-givings, succession feasts, and other inter-group relationships, continued to meet regularly to co-ordinate purely Native affairs – at least those not prohibited by law or by missionaries.[26] Indeed, Tsimshian laws concerning name-giving, inheritance, funerals, and weddings continued to exist well into the twentieth century.

Native names were hereditary, linking the bearer to the past. Duncan and Crosby assigned Christian names to all of the citizens, and, by 1880, there were few Native names left on the church rolls, and few were retained as surnames. But the Tsimshian did not consider the new names as hereditary property for lineage purposes, and, while surnames were passed on from the father's side, hereditary names continued to be inherited from the mother's family. The school records became very confusing because each person had a number of appellations. Laws governing proper forms of address continued to be used and terms such as Mr. and Mrs. were not.[27]

The property rights entailed in hereditary positions were also maintained. Both the missionaries and the later Indian agents attempted to replace lineage possession with individual title, urging each family unit to live on a single lot with exclusive rights to buy or sell. Furthermore, inheritance was supposed to become patrilineal,

1 Port Simpson, 1872
2 Methodist church, built in 1876, burnt down in 1932

3 Mission house with church behind, N.D.
4 Thomas Crosby with Native woman, 'Queen Victoria,' N.D.

5 Port Simpson, 1884
6 Panoramic view of Port Simpson, 1884
7 Thomas Crosby and family, Port Simpson, N.D.

8 Mission school children and teachers, including girls from Crosby Girls' School and Home, N.D., on church steps. Top left, Thomas Crosby; top right, Mrs. Hargrave, teacher; second row, left, Henry Tate, Tsimshian interpreter and assistant teacher

9 Scene at Port Simpson, N.D.

10 Chief Dudoward's residence, 'Eagle House,' designed from pictures of homes back east, N.D.

11 Volunteers at Port Simpson, on beach at Rose Island, N.D.
12 Crosby Girls' Home, Thomas Crosby and Miss Agnes Knight (matron) on verandah, Emma Crosby, far left, 1888
13 'Canadian Girls in Training,' Port Simpson, 1890

14 Crosby Girls' Home and School, built in 1892, burnt down in 1921
15 General Hospital, Port Simpson, built in 1892, demolished in 1946, Dr. Bolton in charge
16 Port Simpson totem poles, 1900

17 Hudson's Bay Company boats at Port Simpson on Portland Canal near the Nass River, 1900
18 Scene from Port Simpson, circa 1915, showing the persistence of Native culture and traditions almost twenty years after Crosby's departure

19 Thomas Crosby and wife Emma, circa 1914, just before his death

with rights going to the widow and children rather than to the lineage males associated with the house head. All those who had contributed money and aid to the building of a house were suddenly deprived of their rights. The successor to the man's name had no claim to what, traditionally, was his by right. While the Tsimshian gave up much of the ceremonialism and potlatching associated with property inheritance, they attempted to cling to the succession laws, and widows often sold property to their husband's successors for a nominal fee.[28] As in the fur-trade period, inheritance remained matrilineal. Furthermore, if there were no successors, adoption would take place. Passing on the inheritance to one's own legal children remained taboo among many Methodist Tsimshian. Daughters would be adopted as sisters if sisters had no male heirs. Lewis Grey went so far as to adopt his wife as sister since he had no sisters or nieces, and his daughter thus became his niece, allowing the inheritance to pass on legally.[29] While, to the missionaries, such actions often seemed ludicrous, these laws were too sacred for the Tsimshian, even as Christians, to violate.

The same laws remained in force for funerals as well. While potlatching was forbidden, relatives maintained their obligations to the dead person, gifts were distributed to those to whom they were due, and titles and privileges were transmitted to the appropriate heirs. Garfield records the process involved in the funerals of such leading Methodists as Herbert Wallace, and, interestingly, points out that the church and its affiliated organizations were often the recipients of gifts that were distributed in a manner analogous to the old potlatch system.[30] Particularly frustrating to Crosby was the Tsimshian law of exogamy. He bemoaned the fact that he had never been able to break it down, since he felt it prevented many potentially good marriages. The decline of some phratries made it difficult for the Tsimshian to obtain what Crosby thought were suitable companions. The first couple to marry within a phratry, he reported, became the object of ill-feeling for a long time, and if such a marriage failed, the Tsimshian blamed it on the violation of the endogamy taboo.[31] The custom by which a man and his friends gave gifts to the prospective bride and her relatives as a contract leading to marriage also continued. The first marriage Crosby performed at Port Simpson involved a misunderstanding in this area. After the couple had been married, it was discovered that another man and his friends had distributed gifts and, thus, expected the woman to become the former's wife. Crosby told them they were 'silly' because in his country if a man gave presents, expecting to marry a woman, he would not complain if she married someone else but would try to find another woman and be 'ashamed to admit the presents.' To this the Tsimshian had replied, 'Oh sir, you needn't talk about your people. We must have these presents back or there will be trouble.' At a subsequent meeting, the council ordered the gifts to be returned.[32]

As noted earlier, Crosby attempted to substitute various bands, organizations, celebrations, and groups for the old Tsimshian feasts. Yet even the replacements took on characteristics that frequently disappointed him. Christmas and New Year's Day were introduced as occasions for big new celebrations replacing the old customs. Elaborate preparations for decorations, gift-giving, and carol-singing began many weeks before Christmas. On Christmas Day, the whole village would be lit up and the evening spent in worship services. This would signal a whole week of celebration. Crosby described it thus: 'The week is spent by the people in inviting each other to their houses. Indeed, this is carried on to a great extent. Much of it very kind and innocent, but it leaves them poor and is not always a help to their spiritual growth.'[33] On New Year's Day, all the companies – the fire company with its brass band, the rifle company, the village council, and the temperance society – gave displays following the New Year's Eve 'watch meeting.' The missionary's unease mounted over the years as the gift-giving and distribution of wealth increased during the Christmas celebrations and also at such events as weddings, name-givings, house-buildings, and funerals.[34] Clearly, the old potlatch mechanisms continued to be operative in the Christian setting.

The persistence of such forms indicates that the process of conversion was not as simple as Crosby had hoped it would be. Converting the Tsimshian to Christianity meant, for Crosby, conversion to a new culture and way of life. Initially, Native people were eager to establish new forms of living and working, and eagerly sought conversion. But retention of old ways was inevitable, as they did not make the same connection between traditional customs and heathenism as did the missionaries. Yet it is important to note that their conversion to Christianity was sincere, and, despite the often unconscious retention of centuries-old customs, they made every effort to adopt the trappings of Western society; hence, their eagerness to build new houses, schools, streets, and churches. It was easier to adopt these trappings than to change those patterns of living, which, to them, were very personal and were often seen as part of the natural order of things. It was one thing to build a new house, for example, but quite another to marry someone from one's own phratry. Even if the missionaries could make them believe that the taboo was invalid, their personal revulsion at such conduct remained. The missionaries failed to realize this distinction and, instead, saw Tsimshian resistance to some elements of change as evidence of residual heathenism.

The Tsimshian were not as aware of their retention of old patterns as was Crosby. Up to about 1885 there was a general understanding among them that they had forsaken old ways and had become good Christian Canadians, despite the fact that many of the marriage, funeral, and inheritance laws were retained. On the outside, with their clothing, schools, houses, organizations, and church, they had become like other Canadians and were proud of their new status. However, external appearances were indicative neither of complete inner change nor of the true status of Native people in Canada. Initially, the Tsimshian believed they had accepted a new way and were now well on the way to full Canadian citizenship. It was not until the middle of the 1880s that they began to realize that their conception of their place in Canadian society did not match the reality of their situation.

Alexander Sutherland made a tour of Port Simpson in 1885, and his interviews with Tsimshian revealed a general state of despondency. One of them, David Swanson, complained that although it had been eleven years since 'we gave up our old way, no one has visited us to help us in anything connected with the improvement of our village.' He pointed out that the people had given all their money for a new church, church bell, roads, new houses, and a 500-foot bridge. They had done all this themselves, and 'now money is scarce because we can get no work, and we need help.'[35] Most informants concurred with this testimony and added that they were upset because Crosby's workload often kept him away and prevented the kind of training they felt they needed. Despite the tremendous improvements that they had made by themselves, they acutely felt the need to have someone instruct them in trades and to train Native missionaries. They clearly felt lost: 'You have opened God's word to us ... and our hearts are happy. We want you to lead us in other things. In old times we had a way of our own; but we have put that away, and want to follow in the way that is taught us ... We are afraid of ourselves, and hardly know what to do.'[36] Chief Albert Nelson reported that although not all things had gone as they had expected, they were not sorry they had followed the Methodists. However, he complained that the kind of improvements they had hoped for were not completed: 'We would like a missionary who could teach our children all things [trades, etc.] ... Mr. Crosby does not stay at home; he goes to visit other places.'[37]

The Tsimshian realized that their poverty was a result of the demands made by their new lifestyle. Crosby's coming had prompted and encouraged the many changes in their village but had not provided the means to pay for them. As a result, the Tsimshian were forced to travel extensively to earn enough to support their new standards, which, therefore, required an ever-increasing dependence on the wage economy. The Tsimshian request for training in trades must be seen in this context, for as Matthew Shepherd told Sutherland: 'As soon as summer comes, everybody is gone. We hope there will be some labour or other means to keep our people at home. The work of God loses by the people being scattered. The people often talk about this. They hope some one will come to teach trades.'[38] No doubt the model of self-sufficient Metlakatla, fifteen miles away, gave a concrete basis to their frustrations.[39] Tsimshian discontent was not based upon a hankering for the old ways but, rather, on an unfulfilled desire to live in a manner similar to White Christians in other parts of Canada and to their friends and relatives at Metlakatla.

Despite the frustration with their missionary and with unfulfilled desires, the Tsimshian wished to continue along the path they had chosen – but with stronger leadership. Initially, they voluntarily accepted tutelage under their missionary leaders. By the end of the 1880s, however, there was a dramatic shift in attitude, and they wanted to have more power over their own destinies. More than anything else, the impetus for this movement was provided by their relations with the provincial and federal governments and the handling of the land issue. This issue was and remains the single most important source of tension between the Native people of British Columbia and the federal and provincial governments.[40]

During the late 1880s and into the 1890s, the Tsimshian began to see clearly, for the first time, that the governments of Canada would always treat them as second-class citizens and not respect their rights or wishes. In 1876, the two levels of government reached an agreement, based on a suggestion by William Duncan, that a commission be appointed to allocate reserves on the basis of each tribe's particular situation rather than on a set acreage. The federal government gave up the idea of extinguishing land title in British Columbia both because of the probable expense and because it already had enough trouble with the 'spoilt child of confederation.' As long as the Native people remained quiet, the federal government was not inclined to raise the issue.[41] This solution also avoided confrontation with the provincial government, which had jurisdiction over provincial Crown lands. But, more importantly, it guaranteed that the two levels of government would throw the problem of Native land title back and forth while the Native people endlessly waited.

Acculturation: 'Secular' Life

In the latter part of the 1880s, officials from both levels of government accused the missionaries on the Northwest Coast of stirring up the Native people over the question of rights to the land. However, as Pollard reported in 1874 (when he first came to Port Simpson), Native people were already concerned about their land rights.[42] Soon after his arrival, scarcely half a year later, Crosby wrote that 'we need the land reserve question settled here, and hope that the Native Commission will visit us soon, and let us know where the Native land is to be; then we hope the people will build a better class of house.'[43] A year later, he stated that the real fears of the Native people arose from rumours that they were to be driven from their land.[44] The missionary, A.E. Green, noted the same feeling when he came to the Nass in 1877. He had heard about the land question from Pollard in 1874 and found the Native people to be worried about White encroachment on their land. He even took a delegation to Victoria in the early 1880s but Powell refused to hear him. Green claimed that, at this time, he had had to restrain the Native people from engaging in violence.[45] The concern over the land question in this region clearly predated the arrival of Methodist missionaries.

The land question attracted widespread public attention in 1876, when Governor-General Lord Dufferin visited Metlakatla and Port Simpson, and stated that the government of Canada did not distinguish between citizens on the basis of race or colour, but was determined to have justice for all. He asserted that Canada was proud of its Native people, and that

> she recognizes them as the ancient inhabitants of the country. The white men have not come amongst you as conquerors but as friends. We regard you as our fellow-subjects, and as equal to us in the eyes of the law as you are in the eye of God, and equally entitled with the rest of the community to the benefits of good government and the opportunity of earning an honest livelihood.[46]

Later that year, while addressing the provincial government about the railroad question, he added a postscript on the land question, stating that he found the neglect of recognizing and extinguishing Native title reprehensible. Incorrectly, he asserted that this was the policy that all the provincial and federal governments in Canada had followed. Dufferin claimed that

> before we touch an acre we make a treaty with the chiefs representing the bands we are dealing with and having agreed upon and paid the stipulated price, often times arrived at after a great deal of haggling and

difficulty, we enter into possession, but not until then do we consider that we are entitled to deal with an acre.[47]

He warned that the current policy of regarding all land as Crown land could result in confrontation between Native people and White settlers.

The Tsimshian rallied around these views and became even more optimistic about the future of their land when Indian Superintendent Powell visited them in July of 1879. The big concerns among the Native people, stated Powell, were that their fishing sites on the Nass and Skeena be preserved and that their village sites not be denied due to the Hudson's Bay Company claiming that land. Powell told them that he felt 'that the Native houses at Fort Simpson are built upon land outside of the Company's limit,' but that, if he was wrong, he was sure that a suitable deal would be arranged. He felt that it would be a pity, in light of the civilized state of the Native people and their trust in the government's protection,

> if their wishes were not gratified. There is no available land at Fort Simpson for them, and I doubt if 10 acres of arable soil for garden purposes can be found in the whole place. Except in view of the railroad developments it is of no present or prospective value to the Company, but to the Native inhabitants it has long been their home.[48]

He also felt that the village council was a 'model of local responsible government,' and he was very impressed with 'their intelligence and shrewd business capacity.'

A few weeks later Crosby wrote Powell mentioning that the Tsimshian were alarmed at the possibility of the Canadian Pacific Railway taking their land away. Crosby stated that the Native people wished to have the whole Tsimshian Peninsula, and, if the railway came to the area, the government could sell the land for the former's benefit. He also mentioned that Whites were beginning to settle in Port Simpson Bay and felt that this was a 'great mistake' because the land question was not yet settled. Powell replied that Indian Reserve Commissioner G.M. Sproat would soon be up there and that he, Crosby, should not 'propose for them or to them what they are to have, as their claims will have every consideration, and your suggestions will embarrass the commission.'[49]

Tsimshian hopes for recognition of their claim to land title were dashed in October of 1881, when the new Indian Reserve Commissioner, Peter O'Reilly, was sent, without notification, to lay out reserves for them. Few Tsimshian were at home at the time, and, at a meeting on 5 October, they handed O'Reilly a written petition stating that they wanted the whole Tsimshian Peninsula between Work's Canal and Chatham Sound, and all the fishing stations on the Nass and Skeena. O'Reilly told them that the government wished to be liberal, but that he 'considered this application unreasonable' and would not give such a large area 'of country of no practicable use to them.'[50] Later he claimed that he made no reserve without their consultation and had included every plot for cultivation and every fishing station asked for – a total of 73,123 acres. He admitted that the Hudson's Bay Company property, on which the Tsimshian had built houses, could become a problem, but he had told the Native people that Powell had made no promises about the land.[51]

Half a year later, the chiefs at Port Simpson addressed a letter to O'Reilly, penned by Crosby, stating that the land given in the reserves was worthless, that the whole country between the Nass and Skeena had been theirs from time immemorial, and that no treaty had extinguished their 'ancient rights.' They offered a counterproposal which would increase their reserve, and, if all else failed, they desired the whole Tsimshian Peninsula and fishing sites on the Nass and Skeena. Crosby mailed a copy of this letter to the Superintendent-General of Indian Affairs along with one of his own, in which he documented other cases in the province where Native land had simply been pre-empted by Whites. He recalled that Lord Dufferin had stated that treaties had always been made, but, at Port Simpson, O'Reilly had neither consulted the Tsimshian nor respected their wishes. He added: 'Apparently they are the very last party whose interests are to be considered.'[52] Powell, a short time later, informed the Superintendent-General of Indian Affairs that the Tsimshian had enough land as well as the most important fishing and village sites. The whole peninsula would amount to 250-300,000 acres and 'is neither required or desired in addition to the allotment Mr. O'Reilly has already made.'[53] According to Powell, the Native people of British Columbia were generally well-cared for, and Crosby's charges of White pre-emption of Native lands were unfounded.

Powell's denial of White encroachment on Native lands became somewhat hollow when, a short time later, articles in the *Daily Colonist*, beginning on 6 May 1883, revealed some strange goings-on at Port Simpson. Apparently, in 1879, a number of White land speculators had applied for land at Port Simpson pending the completion of the Canadian Pacific Railway. The Department of Indian Affairs objected and, despite the fact that it publicly denied Native title, on 3 August placed a freeze on all land around Port Simpson until such time as reserves for the Tsimshian had been established.[54] This action was not, however, published in the *Gazette*, as it should have been.[55] In 1881, O'Reilly laid out the reserve but excluded the land desired by the Whites, doubtless being aware of what land they wanted. The land was then theoretically available for sale in 1882, but the freeze was not removed until 30 March 1883 and was not announced in the *Gazette* until 10 May, four days after the *Daily Colonist* had revealed that the Commissioner of Lands and Works, William Smithe, had given a Mr. Ralph and John Work inside information that the freeze was to be lifted. Before the end of March, Ralph was already up at Port Simpson surveying sites for himself. In April, both Ralph and Work purchased land at Port Simpson. A committee set up by the government to investigate this transaction concluded that because the freeze had been placed on the land secretly and also lifted secretly, 'legally speaking there never was a freeze on the land at all and therefore no action of this government was necessary.'[56] The lack of notification in the *Gazette* in both instances had simply been departmental errors. Yet land desired by Whites had been left out of the Tsimshian reserve by O'Reilly and secretly made available to the friends of the Commissioner of Lands and Works.

To the Tsimshian, this action became known as the 'land grab.' As Louis Gosnell stated later, Powell's visit had given them a feeling that he would protect their interests: 'We thought those words were true. Not long after a land surveyor came here, and we wished to know what he had come for. Afterwards we found out he had come to secretly mark out land for white chiefs, some say Government chiefs.'[57] Alfred Dudoward claimed that Powell's name was 'on a post among the pre-emptors around the harbour. Instead of helping us he is making money out of Tsimshian land.'[58] The Tsimshian at Port Simpson no longer believed that the governments had their best interests at heart. To add insult to injury, J.W. MacKay was appointed to act as Indian agent despite the fact that Native people had clearly indicated that they had no desire to have one. There was a growing awareness in Victoria that the Port Simpson and Metlakatla Natives were not going to be easily persuaded out of their firm convictions about their rights, and it was hoped that an Indian agent could calm things down.[59]

MacKay's efforts were doomed from the start. The Tsimshian told him emphatically that they did not want an agent, and, during a long meeting with him on 8 December 1883, they set forth their views on their treatment by the government. They appealed to the common element of Christianity which they supposedly shared with the Queen and the government. Arthur Wellington argued that if the

Queen and government were under God's law, as MacKay said they were, how could the present situation be? He asked, 'Did you ever see a Christian take land from another Christian, and sell it, not letting him know anything about it?'[60] This was what they saw happening, and, because they were Christian, they did not fight back. In 1857, Duncan had brought news of their liberty and, added Wellington, 'I have read in God's book, the Bible, that the poor are not despised in God's sight.'[61]

Alfred Dudoward added to this testimony by questioning the old and respected Paul Legaic as to whether England and Native people had ever been at war, whether the English had bought the land, whether Native people had given the land to the Queen, or whether the English had stolen it. Upon receiving a negative reply to each query, he reported that they would claim the land until the issue was settled. MacKay told them that Powell and O'Reilly had informed him that all had been settled. But Dudoward, using Lord Dufferin's speech as the foundation for his argument, replied that it had not been settled. At the end of the meeting, MacKay informed them that he would recommend a treaty and would convey their desires to the proper authorities. That was the last the Tsimshian heard from him. Early in 1884, A.C. Elliott was appointed as a stipendiary magistrate with authority to act as an Indian agent, but he would be paid only under the former position.

As the tensions between the governments and Native people increased, government officials became convinced that the Tsimshian were not acting on their own behalf but as 'mouthpieces' for Duncan and Crosby. In December of 1883, MacKay advised Powell that the missionaries should be restrained from giving all secular advice as they, generally, 'are men of extreme views and are neither competent to sustain a governmental policy, nor to properly direct the Native mind in matters involving questions of law and justice.'[62] He blamed the present state of unrest on the missionaries. It would seem that government officials never took the Native people seriously because they saw them as childlike and, thus, were convinced that the missionaries were the instigators of such complicated notions as aboriginal rights and land claims.[63] Indeed, the blame for any problems could only reside with their advisers – the missionaries.

The Metlakatla Inquiry of 1884, called to investigate the problem between Duncan and Ridley, concluded that one of the most vexing areas of dispute was the notion of land title, which had to be 'checked by the assertion of authority,' or it would cause serious problems all over the Northwest Coast. The root of the problem was Lord Dufferin's visit and his remarks, which were foreign to his mission and 'have been sedulously inculcated in the Native mind by some of the missionaries who appear to have been ignorant of the constitutional law upon the subject.'[64] The danger was that the Tsimshian would not accept the Indian Advancement Act or the Indian agent, who, as Alexander Davie told them, was appointed to take care of them. Davie added, 'Indian agents are for the good of Native people. The Indian agents tell us what the Native people want.'[65] Apparently it was not sufficient when the Native people themselves told the governments what they wanted.

The issue came to a head, in 1886, when Duncan's followers removed some surveyors from Metlakatla, forcing them to stop work. Crosby advised his followers not to make trouble as he believed that the issue could be settled amicably. But, as he wrote John Robson, it was hard to hold the people back when they were convinced that the surveys would reduce their lands and it appeared that no one was defending their rights. He advised Robson, then Commissioner of Lands and Works, to resurvey the area and to appoint a commission including people who would 'look at the matter from the Native standpoint.' As well, advance notice should be given so that the people could be at home and say what they wanted to say. He concluded, 'The people act like men contending for what they believe to be their legal rights and I hope they will be dealt with in such a way as to bring about confidence and good will among all the parties.'[66]

Duncan and his followers, weary of battling Bishop Ridley and the two levels of government, decided, by November 1886, to search for a new home in Alaska.[67] It became apparent to Duncan that the government would always take the side of the Church Missionary Society and would not recognize Native title. The Port Simpson people decided that it was time once more to pursue legal channels and attempt to soften the government position. Contrary to the view of Powell and Deputy Superintendent-General of Indian Affairs Vankoughnet, who said that Native people were merely acting on Crosby's orders, the Tsimshian, including Nishga and Gitksan leaders, had to persuade a reluctant Crosby to accompany them to Victoria to speak to the government about their claims.[68] When they got to Victoria, after a difficult trip in the middle of winter, the Tsimshian were informed that no White interpreters were permitted. Charles Burton was told that the 'government wanted to hear his story from his own lips,'[69] even though he insisted that his English was poor.

The meetings occurred on 3 and 8 February. The substance of the Tsimshian position was that they wished to be free on the land and have their rights guaranteed by a treaty. Smithe quickly dismissed the demand for a treaty after the Tsimshian had told him that evidence for the making of treaties was in law-books but were unable to tell him which specific book. Smithe replied that he knew of no such book in England or Canada. The Tsimshian, he said, had been misled. Smithe countered their desire to be free on the land by arguing that the difference between Native people and Whites 'is that being still Indians, or ... in the position of children, you are not permitted, so far, to exercise the franchise ... you are like children. We don't give our children the right to vote until they have come to manhood – to be taught to read and write and think properly.'[70] Whenever they learned these skills they could pre-empt land – not communally but individually. The Tsimshian were also told that reservations could be extended if there were omissions, but that hunting grounds would not be added because, as Smithe pointed out, they appeared to be anxious to rise beyond their past and such a wish was 'mere sentiment.' Rather, they could get licences and hunt wherever Whites were allowed to hunt. The same was true for mining and lumbering. But all the land belonged to the Queen and she never gave land to White settlers when they moved into an area nor did she give them reserves – they had to pay for the land. Thus, Native people were more fortunate. The Queen only gave land to them because 'they do not know so well how to make their own living ... and special indulgence is extended to them and special care shown.'[71]

Charles Burton's simple reply to all this was that the land was theirs, and that, by Native laws, every chief had his own hunting and fishing area. O'Reilly then pointed out that such a request would mean giving Native people the whole country, although he did say that he would add land if he had omitted some important areas due to some of the people not being at home during his previous visit. Burton replied that they had not come to quibble about boundaries but wanted to be free on the land, with a treaty guaranteeing their rights, so that it could not be taken from them like it had been from the 'flatheads' in Victoria. Their position was not one of defiance. They wanted to have the same rights under British law as did the Whites.

> Some of the Native people now are able to be like a white man – almost like white men, only they are not allowed to be yet. This is the very reason that I have come myself; and I am very glad to see you and speak to you that we are everyday growing and trying to be like white men; but the way we are fixed now we don't know the land is ours, and have not got anything to show that it is. We are not free on the land; we

cannot build on it; we are liable to be removed, as we have heard, the way things are now.[72]

Crosby was disappointed with the nature of the interview, feeling that the Tsimshian had not been able to say what they had wanted or in the way they had wanted. He felt that the government had not taken their requests seriously: 'I think they just threw the dust in their eyes by saying they were good men and they had made good speeches [sic] but I do not see what good it will do.'[73] Nevertheless, there was some optimism, as the government had promised to send a commission out to Port Simpson to investigate the problem. If the Tsimshian had known that the commission was a token gesture by the government, their optimism would probably have vanished. On 27 May 1887, John A. Macdonald stated, in a letter to the Privy Council, that the Port Simpson and Nass Natives were well-disposed, and the 'appointment of a Commission such as that proposed ... would tend to conserve good feeling on the part of the Native people.'[74]

Any 'good feeling' disappeared in the summer of 1887, when surveyors came to Port Simpson to complete the surveys before the commission had heard the Tsimshian. To add further insult, the commission, consisting of federal appointee Clement J. Cornwall, and provincial appointee J.B. Planta, arrived in Port Simpson in the middle of October 1887, when few Tsimshian were at home. Only forty Native people attended their meeting, and the commissioners noted a general air of despondency. Despite the civilized appearance of the village, the Tsimshian drew the commissioners' attention to the general state of disrepair of the roads and bridges, saying it was due to the 'uncertainty of their future.' The only grounds for such a feeling, answered the commissioners, was Tsimshian opposition to governmental control under the Indian Advancement Act.

The commissioners had been instructed to 'be careful to discountenance ... any claim of Native title to Provincial lands.'[75] As this was the heart of Tsimshian grievances, there was little likelihood that the commission would satisfy them. The commission saw itself simply as an instrument to record Native views and then reaffirm the positions of their respective governments.

Tsimshian complaints centred largely around the land question. They complained bitterly that the government had sent surveyors before sending the commission. The land had been theirs from time immemorial. They were willing to give the government large tracts of land (equivalent to 160 acres per person at Port Simpson), but it was imperative that they keep the Tsimshian Peninsula and the

Skeena and Nass fisheries and hunting stations. Regarding the latter river, the Tsimshian noted that the land behind the river, traditionally theirs, had been given to Anglican Natives under the leadership of Ridley, and traditional village sites and graveyards had been destroyed. They further complained about the Hudson's Bay Company land as well as the 'land grab' around the harbour, for which they had received no money.

Another area of contention was the abolition of their village council by Magistrate A.C. Elliott. The current disrepair in the village was linked to this act, as the council no longer had any power: 'These councillors were the strength of the village; they can't do anything now.'[76] The Tsimshian stated that their demand for a village council was not an act of defiance against the Canadian government. Rather, they wanted Canadian laws but felt that the laws of the Indian Advancement Act would keep them backward, when they actually wanted to be like Whites. As David Leask had said in 1883, the Tsimshian had advanced beyond the provisions of the Indian Advancement Act: 'It would be like trying to put a small pair of shoes on feet too large for them. It would only cramp our feet and prevent us from walking as fast as we did without such regulations.'[77] While other Native people might possibly benefit from this Act, the Port Simpson Tsimshian were beyond it. In addition, the agents sent by the government, particularly Elliott, did not stop the Hudson's Bay Company from selling liquor – indeed, he sold it himself.

In their evaluation of the situation, the commission reported that the problem was a continuation of the policy established by Duncan. The missionaries were not exerting their influence to convince the Tsimshian to submit to the government.

> In conjunction with this has arrived the time at which the Native people having acquired a little mental activity and a very partial knowledge of some of the things about which they are agitating, probably imagine that they know a great deal and are thoroughly able to say what is good for themselves.
>
> So in a way that would not call for particular attention were it not seriously intended, they hold themselves as above and beyond the existing laws which affect them as Indians.[78]

The commissioners saw it as imperative that the Tsimshian be brought under the Indian Advancement Act and have an agent to 'aid' and 'instruct' them 'as to the objects and purport of the law' and place them under the control of 'civil power.'[79] The commission concluded that 'in past years the Native people of the North-West Coast have been left too much alone, almost isolated, from proper governmental regulation and control.'[80]

The Tsimshian were not at all pleased with these conclusions or with the manner in which the commission had gathered information. They had appointed Alfred Dudoward as their chief speaker, and, in the middle of his address, the commissioners had adjourned for the day and then refused to hear the rest of the speech the following day because he was only a 'half-breed.' Furthermore, the Tsimshian had not been allowed to respond to Cornwall's closing remarks. Instead, they had sent a letter to the commission, but it was not included in the report. Their anger was further kindled when the government went ahead and appointed Charles Todd as Indian agent and S.Y. Wooton as stipendiary magistrate. On 5 January 1888, they sent an angry letter to Todd advising him to stay away from their village. They reminded him of the situation at Metlakatla, and, since the governments never responded to their letters, indicated: 'We do not wish to have anything done 'till our land is settled.'[81]

The issue assumed a denominational character when Cornwall, an Anglican, contrasted the Church Missionary Society with Methodist missionaries. The former, he said, respect the law, and, as a result, the Native people at Metlakatla and Kincolith[82] wanted the Indian Advancement Act. The Methodists, who were not men 'of high class' or 'of education,'

> find themselves in a position which enables them to exercise great authority and control over the Native people. This upsets them; they lose command of themselves and in their desire to retain that authority and control, they do not, to say the least of it, strenuously combat the worst instincts of the Native people with reference to their temporal interests.[83]

He felt that the Tsimshian needed different leadership. Their demands had been articulated by the missionaries because they themselves had no idea of property. Except for their homes, 'the beasts of the field have as much ownership in the land as he does.'[84]

The *Daily Colonist* entered the fray in May when it reported that the missionaries had misled the Native people regarding title and opposition to the Indian Advancement Act because the former did not want to lose control of the latter's councils. The Tsimshian at Port Simpson had been treated generously, and besides, Sir John A. Macdonald was the Superintendent-General of Indian Affairs, and 'does it stand to reason that he would permit the existence of such a deplorable state of affairs as the missionaries recite, if brought to his notice?'[85] A short time later another letter appeared in the paper signed 'Not a Methodist' in which the writer was highly critical of the provincial and federal governments' handling of the Metlakatla and Port Simpson situations. He felt that there was a conflict of interest in sending commissions made up exclusively of Anglicans to settle issues, particularly because the Anglican Church's criticism of Duncan and the Methodists was based solely on differing religious positions or affiliations. These missionaries were not the source of the Native land title issue. Rather, the writer concluded, Tsimshian desire for recognition of their land title was based on Lord Dufferin's 1876 speeches.[86]

Both the provincial and federal governments blamed the missionaries for the unrest and became increasingly alarmed that they might mislead the public into believing that Native affairs were being mismanaged. Nowhere else in British Columbia, they noted, did these issues arise. On 12 June 1888, Todd advised Powell that Crosby and Green should be removed and steps taken to compel 'respect for law and government supremacy which has been almost destroyed amongst these Native people by these cunning disloyal ... [men].'[87] This sentiment was shared by the Department of Indian Affairs in Ottawa, which felt that Crosby's and Green's removal was the only workable solution to the problem of Native unrest.

What government authorities could not see was the Native role in the problem. Most significantly, Alfred Dudoward, selected by the village council to articulate its position to the commission, was not even a church member in 1887, illustrating quite clearly that the Tsimshian were not acting on behalf of the missionaries. Furthermore, Dennis Jennings, in a letter to Ebenezer Robson on 15 January 1889, felt that the Tsimshian could benefit from the Indian Advancement Act because the lack of a village council prevented village improvement. However, less than a month later, he reported that he felt that the Native people had just demands which the government could easily redress.[88] The missionaries were not dictating the action on the land question.

Meanwhile, the Tsimshian heard nothing from either government about the results of the commission. In a most revealing statement, Vankoughnet, of the federal Department of Indian Affairs, noted that he had not felt the need to respond to the Tsimshian because the commission was a provincial one, as was the question at issue. All citizens had to obey the law of the land, he argued, and for Native people the law was the Indian Act. He conveyed his understanding of the issue to his underlings, instructing them to inform Indian

Agent Todd of his position. Todd, in turn, was to tell the Tsimshian.[89] However, it appears that the message got lost in transmission; in any case, the Tsimshian never got it.

Instead, Indian Land Commissioner O'Reilly went out once again, and, by October, completed reserves for the Tsimshian that were approved by 1 April 1888. As one hundred of the Metlakatla Natives under Bishop Ridley wanted the Indian Advancement Act, it was deemed necessary to divide the reserve between those who wanted the Act and those who did not. What particularly annoyed the Port Simpson Natives, numbering over 700, was the fact that the reserve was divided into equal halves and, furthermore, that Metlakatla had also been chosen as the site for a new industrial school, something the former had been requesting for years. They were convinced that they were being punished for being Methodists. As usual, protests got nowhere, and Crosby decided to take the whole affair to Ottawa, armed with affidavits and statements from the Tsimshian and other witnesses.

In this venture, Crosby had the support of most of his Methodist colleagues and superiors.[90] At the ministerial sessions from 1887-92, there was unanimous condemnation of the governments' handling of the land question. In 1888, and again in 1889, the British Columbia Conference passed a special resolution which 'strongly disapproved' of the policies of the two levels of government, particularly because they seemed to discriminate against their missionaries. They recommended that the General Board of Missions of the Methodist Church send its own commission to investigate the issue and lay it before the Department of Indian Affairs.[91] They felt that there was a strong need to restore the good feeling of the governments towards the Methodists and to end discriminatory practices, for, while the Methodists did receive aid for education in the form of per capita grants, any other requests for assistance were turned down.

In April of 1889, Crosby and a delegation of leading Methodists met with government officials in Ottawa to refute the charges that they were inciting the Native people. They noted that the land question had been bothering the Tsimshian even before the Methodists had arrived at Port Simpson. Shortly after this meeting, at the request of the Department of Indian Affairs, they presented the Superintendent-General of Indian Affairs with a lengthy letter containing the statements and affidavits which Crosby had gathered before he had left Port Simpson.

The letter summarized all the Native grievances that had accumulated over the years.[92] Mention was also made of Duncan's visit to Ottawa in 1885, when he met with John A. Macdonald. However, the

Tsimshian had received no official reply from him concerning the matters which had been brought to his attention. Herbert Wallace, a Tsimshian chief, reported that the visit had led to a guarantee from Macdonald that the land was theirs and that nobody would be allowed to take it from them. Later he had met Vankoughnet, Deputy Superintendent-General of Indian Affairs, in Victoria and had asked him why they had received no reply. Vankoughnet had told him that O'Reilly had advised him that the Tsimshian were happy, to which Wallace had replied that he was a Tsimshian and he was not happy at all. Vankoughnet could not understand why the Tsimshian wanted so much land and felt that Duncan had put them up to it. But Wallace had replied that Duncan was in Alaska and that he, Wallace, was here 'because you did not do what you promised.'[93] The Tsimshian also noted that when the Hudson's Bay Company first settled at Port Simpson, it came at Legaic's invitation. The land was theirs and the Hudson's Bay Company would have had no reason to come to the area 'if we had not been here.'[94] Arthur Wellington Clah compared the Port Simpson situation to that of Ahab and Naboth; God had not been pleased then and he was not pleased with the government now.[95] Several Tsimshian intimated that they had spoken to the governor of Alaska and were ready to follow their brothers and sisters out of British Columbia to an area where they could get decent schooling with proper government support.

The Methodist Church added to this testimony by pointing out that the government allowed 'charges of the most gross and libellous description' to be made against their missionaries. They felt that discrimination against their church was unfair because the root of the problem was government policy. James Douglas had always extinguished title before allowing settlement by Europeans, and Lord Dufferin had stated that this was government policy elsewhere in Canada. The government also did little to enforce potlatch or liquor laws. They complained about their inability to get grants for their schools and industrial shows as well as medicine for their missions. The Tsimshian argument was supported by James Deans, a Presbyterian and long-time resident of the Queen Charlotte Islands. He testified that he saw government discrimination against Methodist missionaries as they could never get supplies and medicines while Anglican missionaries were always well stocked.[96]

In the summer of 1889, Superintendent-General of Indian Affairs Edgar Dewdney went to British Columbia and met with government officials, but nothing was settled, for, as Sutherland wrote Crosby, 'I did not expect that very much would result from Mr. Dewdney's visit to the coast, as it was very evident that he did not desire that we should be in any way represented in the investigation.'[97] By May of 1891, the Department of Indian Affairs had not yet made an official reply to the letter from the Methodist Missionary Society. The only evidence of government awareness of the letter was a secret memorandum between Vankoughnet and Dewdney, dated 3 July 1889, in which Vankoughnet blamed any tensions between the governments and the Tsimshian on the missionaries. He said that any allegations of unfair treatment were unsupported because the Methodists never specified 'the Native people who have been subjected to such unfair treatment, nor the agents who have thus treated them.'[98] The Methodists had brought the current state of tension upon themselves, whereas all Anglican missionaries encouraged their people to adopt the Indian Advancement Act and accept an agent. Douglas's policy could not be used as a precedent because he only made treaties as a representative of the Hudson's Bay Company, and his treaties were made to facilitate trade. Dufferin's speech, furthermore, had been outside of the scope of his visit to British Columbia. The Tsimshian had never been promised acknowledgment of their claims to title – only as much land as could be of possible use to them. Powell had allowed no missionary interpreters in 1887 because the missionaries always gave *their* version of the matters at hand rather than that of the Tsimshian. The industrial school at Metlakatla was not evidence of favouritism as it was non-sectarian, open to all, and run by a Presbyterian. Indeed, Cornwall had found no evidence of favouritism towards the Anglicans or of collusion between them and the government. He felt that the solution to the whole problem was in the hands of the Methodist Missionary Society:

> By simply withdrawing from the points at which the friction between the Missionaries and Agents exists the present representatives of their Body and replacing them by men who will restore in the minds of the Native people confidence in the Government and will advise submission on their part to the laws regulating Native matters within the Dominion as well as obedience to the lawful requirements of the Indian agents placed over them.[99]

Not once did Vankoughnet consider that the Tsimshian themselves might be dissatisfied with the provincial and federal governments' handling of their situation.

Following the failure of the Methodist Missionary Society to get any action, things seemed to quieten down at Port Simpson. Todd reported in August of 1889 that the land agitation was settling down and 'giving place to a feeling of contentment with respect to the Government and a more friendly feeling towards their white neighbours.'[100] Over the next few years, in their annual reports, O'Reilly, Superintendent-General of Indian Affairs A.W. Vowell, and Todd reported that the Tsimshian were happy with the allotted reserves and that the land question had been settled.

This position is difficult to understand and seems to be merely an attempt by the government to give the public the impression that all was well. Indeed, Crosby was silent, and evidence points to minimal involvement on his part in the land question. But Crosby's lack of involvement did not mean that the Tsimshian were happy. In January of 1891, over 200 residents – most of the male population – of Port Simpson signed a letter addressed to Member of Parliament Robert Hanley Hall complaining that the land question had not been settled. They reviewed the whole history of the problem, from Powell's assurance in 1879 to the commission of 1887. They were offended by the fact that, while they had refused an agent, A.C. Elliott, although he came as a judge, also had authority to act as an agent. They were upset that they had never received a reply from the provincial or federal governments to any of their letters, and, while some of their brothers and sisters had gone to Alaska, 'We have not gone yet, and still hope to get our rights and do not wish to shame our government as they did.'[101] But government inaction seemed to be calculated 'to provoke us to break the law.' They saw little good in Indian agents: 'All they do, as far as we can see, is to draw their salary.'[102] They wanted to be like the rest of Canada's citizens, with a simple form of municipal government which would allow them to manage their own affairs. Because they had given up all pagan practices, they did not want a law similar to those who were still heathen and thus needed the Indian Act.

A short time after he received this letter, Hall suggested to Vowell that the Indian Act be changed specifically for the Port Simpson Tsimshian to allow them to elect their own chief officer who would report directly to the Department of Indian Affairs rather than through an agent, allowing them to sell lands which they did not want and to use the money for education or other needs, and giving them the right to pre-empt land.[103] Vankoughnet pointed out, however, that special legislation would have to be passed because Native people were not allowed to pre-empt land, and the other two resolutions were built on this right. He would not recommend such action, adding: 'I may also state that from the feeling known to prevail in the local house it would be useless to attempt legislation at all favourable to the Indians, the sentiment being to curtail the privileges and concessions already granted rather to than in any way increase them.'[104] The significance of this correspondence is not so much in its contents or in the government's response, but rather, in the fact that it was a community effort which bore no evidence of missionary influence. As noted earlier, this was also the period in which the Band of Christian Workers began its drive for control of religious expression. Gone were the days when the Tsimshian would simply follow the leadership of their missionary or of government officials. As Herbert Wallace stated, the Tsimshian dislike the governments because 'they say the Native people are like little children and don't know anything. God does not call those small who keep his Word.' He resented the implication that because they were like little children they did not know how to use the land and that, as a result, the government was cutting it up. The family stones reminded the Tsimshian that the land was theirs, and they could not see why they needed licences to hunt and fish on their own land.[105]

This was also the time when the missionaries decried the resurgence of Native customs. In February of 1890, Green reported that few Native people led 'godly lives,' and that the majority were opposed to 'practical religion.' He felt that the Native people placed too much confidence in their councils and too little in God's word. They seemed to want the liberty to do as they pleased, determining morality by majority vote. The sabbath was also being neglected, there was drinking, and old feasts and potlatching were being revived. In December, he reported, many had attended a large potlatch given by Chief Shakes.[106] That same year, Alfred Dudoward gave a large feast and erected an imposing pole in memory of his dead uncle. The complaints about potlatching, feasting, and ostentatious display continued throughout 1891 and 1892.

The Tsimshian were beginning to replace their small homes with larger, typically Canadian homes, which included sitting-rooms, flower gardens, gravelled driveways, and electricity. Wealth seemed to be on the increase. Todd reported, in 1889, that the Tsimshian earned more than any other Native people on the Coast and also had more expensive tastes. Their chief source of wealth was the salmon industry, although many received a substantial income from the sale of furs, building, lumbering, steam-boating, and manufacturing.[107] There were also a number of Native businesses, and the Department of Indian Affairs noted that Native living quarters and lifestyle rivalled those of the best white communities. Todd's 1894 report also mentioned that the Native people, Japanese, and Whites had successfully struck some canneries for higher wages.[108]

Clearly, the Tsimshian were moving beyond their initial acceptance of White culture as presented to them under the leadership of a paternalistic missionary. They seemed to be striving for and achieving economic and material equality with their fellow White citizens. Yet they lacked political power. Specifically, they desired an elective municipal council to oversee the upgrading of the village as well as the improvement of public utilities and roads. On 23 November 1893, the chiefs of Port Simpson petitioned Todd, asking for 'an elective Native council under the provisions of the Indian Advancement Act [as a] large number believe that the time is come when we should have an organized council.'[109] On 6 November 1894, the Act was applied and elections for a council were held a short time later. By-laws were drawn up by the council to regulate the development of the village as well as to oversee and control the behaviour of the citizens.

Submitting to the Act seemed, on the surface (and to the provincial and federal governments), to indicate Tsimshian acceptance of the rule of the Department of Indian Affairs and an admission of the right of the government to establish reserves; or, put in another way, acknowledgment of the Crown's right to the land. But it was none of these. It was, for one thing, a rejection of missionary advice. After the failure of the 1889 trip to Ottawa, there is little evidence of missionary involvement in the land question or in negotiations over the Indian Advancement Act. Acceptance of a council under the Act meant the end of Crosby's control over village affairs and poignantly illustrated that he, as a secular adviser, no longer had the confidence of the Tsimshian.

Besides showing the rejection of Crosby's power, the establishment of the council was also an attempt by the Tsimshian to gain control over village management. The land issue had not been forgotten nor, as the two levels of government may have thought, was the treatment they had received from the surveyors and commissions. There was a constant battle between Indian agent Todd and the Port Simpson council regarding policy. At the end of 1896, barely two years after they had submitted to the Act, this tension flared up. The council members wrote a letter to Indian Superintendent Vowell, complaining of Todd's ineptitude. They said that a flag promised by Todd never arrived and that a promised survey for new houses was delayed for two years, with the result that the wood bought for this purpose rotted. They added that Todd had not come to see them that winter until after the New Year, and, when he did come, he vetoed their plans for village improvements, got angry, stamped his feet, and said he would wash his hands of their proposals. The previous winter, they noted, he had said that the people were 'worse than dogs,' and, when he refused to take the council's advice to restrain himself, they walked out on him because they did not want to see a recurrence of the violence he had reportedly caused on the Nass.[110]

The council went a step further and wrote a letter to Ottawa outlining the same complaints. They stated that Todd lived twenty miles away and seldom visited. Todd had also done nothing to get them an industrial school and never visited their day schools. Furthermore, he made decisions contrary to the will of the majority and constantly got angry with them.[111] Crosby and Raley supported the Tsimshian position and aided in circulating a petition demanding that Dr. A.E. Bolton be appointed to replace Todd as Indian agent.

Todd defended himself by stating that he had never promised a flag. He had informed the Tsimshian that the government might send one but had added that he had seen little need for one as they already had several. No doubt his rejection of the flag was prompted by his recognition of the nature of Herbert Wallace's tongue in cheek request: 'Now that we have ceased to be rebels and wish to support the government they should send us a large flag.'[112] Todd went on to explain that the surveys for the new homes had, unfortunately, been delayed because government estimates had not allowed for such an expense, but the Tsimshian refused to accept this explanation. Furthermore, the previous winter he had had pneumonia and could not visit Port Simpson until he had recovered. As to his rejection of village council legislation, it had been aimed at crushing the Salvation Army and was thus beyond the scope of the council.[113] He admitted holding back legislation for two years, but he could not allow religious disputes to be settled in this manner. He had told them he would wash his hands of such an attitude, but claimed that he had never called them dogs or stormed out of their council.

The Tsimshian dispute with Todd was not merely a personality clash. Later that year, during conferences with Minister of the Interior Clifford Sifton, the Tsimshian renewed their request for title to the land because, they said, they had been told that they 'did not own an inch of land anywhere.' Their reserve boundaries had repeatedly been altered and they only had one-half of it, while the Metlakatlans, with only one-eighth of the number of people, had the other half. They complained that Vowell, Todd, and O'Reilly never answered their appeals and that Todd never visited them.[114]

Thus Tsimshian acceptance of the Indian Advancement Act was not a sign that they had been defeated by the provincial or federal governments' refusal to deal with their wishes. Rather, they used it to pursue their old grievances and to attain the use of an elective village council which would be independent of their missionary. The council was an attempt to use the system to attain self-government.

Despite the lack of political power, dramatic changes had occurred to their way of life. By the mid-1890s, they were employed in a wide range of activities: 'Salmon canneries, procuring and rafting saw-logs, hunting, fishing, boat-building, trading, working at sawmills and steamboats, cultivating patches of land, carrying freight and passengers from place to place, and by earning money in many other ways through assisting white men at any kind of work.'[115] Visitors and government officials reported that the Tsimshian seemed to be wealthy and to have good, well-furnished houses. Such glowing reports, however, should be tempered by an awareness of the general attitude towards Native people at that time; for many White observers, any sign of Native initiative indicated progress because it defied stereotype.

The Tsimshian were not as enthusiastic about their lot in life. James Woodsworth, representing the Mission Board, visited Port Simpson in 1896 and heard the other side of the story. He reported that one of the wealthiest chiefs with the best house in the village came to him in worn and torn clothes and said 'the people were impoverished by giving to collections.'[116] Others complained that they were poorer than they had been in the past. They said they wanted

> a preacher who would build them a cannery or a steamboat, or a sawmill, or do something to help them along material lines. Further, they wanted their young men to have power, this did not mean spiritual power, but authority, especially in church government. They were impressed with the spectacular and noisy meetings of the Salvation Army.[117]

Woodsworth also mentioned visiting a Band of Christian Workers meeting which, he said, was a noisy, emotional, and demonstrative affair. They complained that they could not use their style of worship in church and that, therefore, many had left for the Salvation Army.

The issue raised by the Tsimshian was not one of wealth, even though it was often presented as such. They had a certain amount of wealth but much of it was acquired by travelling to other parts of the province for employment. What they wanted were their own sources of revenue, in the form of their own canneries, sawmills, and steamers. They wanted the power to control their own destiny, and, as Woodsworth pointed out, 'in church government' as in secular affairs. They did not want to be dependent on others; neither upon Whites for employment nor upon missionaries for religious instruction. More important, their goal seemed to be to participate in White society – using that society's own methods. As Rolf Knight points out, at this particular time in British Columbia history, their role as wage labourers was important.[118] At Port Simpson they wanted to be more than employees.

Port Simpson was also the projected site for a Canadian Pacific Railway line. In the 1890s it became the seat of government and police headquarters for the region. It also became an important stop for steamers and freighters headed for northern British Columbia and Alaska. Further, there was heavy traffic up the Nass and Skeena rivers, and two hotels plied a busy trade. The Tsimshian wanted a greater role in the action.[119]

Crosby's role had thus diminished. The Tsimshian had moved beyond what he or any missionary could offer, and he no longer had the admiration and respect he had enjoyed in earlier years. The Band of Christian Workers, the religious expression of Tsimshian desire for control over their own lives, caused him no end of frustration. During these years he wrote few letters to the missionary periodicals in eastern Canada. Although his methods were probably better suited to primary evangelization, his lessening role was more the result of a rising Tsimshian consciousness than of any methods he might have used. Paternalism was no longer acceptable to the Tsimshian, and any future missionary work would have to be responsive to their wishes.

In 1895, Matthew Johnston wrote a letter to Sutherland, signed by eleven others (including five chiefs), asking for Crosby's replacement. Sutherland wrote Crosby that he had heard rumours of difficulty.

> It may be that the opposition developed is unreasonable, and there may be no good cause for asking for a change. At the same time there are occasions when duty would require us to hold our own interests in abeyance for the sake of the Lord's cause, and when the missionary would do wisely to ask for another field even though he felt that he had given no just cause of complaint.[120]

At the same time he addressed a reply to Matthew Johnston expressing sorrow that the early love for Crosby had gone. Many stories of the past few years had caused him sorrow, especially the fact that the Tsimshian were listening to other teachers. Rather than asking for Crosby's removal, they should pray for him: 'But sometimes a missionary may have been long enough in one place, and then it is good that he should go away, and that another should come.'[121] If they decided that Crosby should go, he hoped they would wish him well and not let him go with a sad heart. A short time later, several of those whose names appeared on the letter said that they had not written it and that it was a forgery. The matter ended there.

Yet Crosby's days at Port Simpson were virtually finished. Information concerning his activities during his last few years there is scarce, but what there is seems to indicate that he was merely attending to administrative and organizational matters. He did travel occasionally, but his relationship to the Port Simpson people seemed tense, especially with regard to matters of worship, the Band of Christian Workers, and the Salvation Army. The hopes and aims that Crosby had represented for the Tsimshian in the early years had not been realized, nor did it appear that they would be.

Tsimshian frustrations revolved around the fact that they could not attain the same rights as the non-Native citizens of British Columbia. They had adopted external features of Western society, such as clothing, shelter, food, social relationships, and even Christianity. But they had also gone one step further and had attempted to adopt many of its cultural values – its way of looking at and behaving in the world. But, and central to the whole issue, they could not become part of that society. They could attempt to think, act, and live like other Canadians, but Canadian society would not accept them even if they could demonstrate that they had forsaken their past in favour of the Western way. While Crosby was not totally to blame for this injustice, he refused to give the Tsimshian power over their religious expression just as the governments refused to give them political power over everyday affairs.

In making their decision to accept Western ways, the Tsimshian had turned their back on a way of life which had integrated religious expressions and the social structure with underlying cultural values. A stable society, according to Clifford Geertz's model, requires that everyday life, social structure, and religious symbols be integrated within a cultural framework. By becoming Western, therefore, it became imperative that the everyday life of the Tsimshian reflect the fact that they were completely integrated into Canadian society. The land issue was the most dramatic, poignant, and painful demonstration of the fact that the rights of full citizenship – a precondition for full participation in Canadian affairs – would not be theirs. Thus, they could not achieve harmony between their new cultural framework, their everyday life, and their social system. Political and economic power, the measure of worth in Canadian society, was not available to the Tsimshian.

Thus, Crosby's paternalism was, in itself, not the reason for the decline of the mission. The real problem lay in the nature of Native/Canadian relations in the late nineteenth century. The land issue, in particular, illustrated the ways in which Native people were expected to act like Canadians and encouraged to reject their past but then refused the alleged benefits which rejection of 'Indian-ness' supposedly entailed. In the late 1880s, and into the 1890s, the Tsimshian began to realize this predicament and Crosby lost much of his influence. Crosby's health began to suffer because of these tensions, and, in 1892, he developed asthma, which plagued him for the rest of his life. While the adventure and romance of mission work remained, Crosby seemed anxious to leave Port Simpson. In 1896 he informed Robson that he would like to go to the Upper Skeena: 'It might be best for my health and there is a grand field up there.'[122] He got his wish in 1897 when he was appointed chairman of the British Columbia Conference of the Methodist Church of Canada, ending twenty-three years at Port Simpson. Robson reported that he left Port Simpson suffering from asthma, a cold, and fatigue.[123]

CHAPTER SIX

The Role of the Tsimshian in Conversion

The interpretation and understanding of the relationship between a missionary and those to whom he ministers is complicated by the differing backgrounds of each party. Because most students of missions share the cultural and intellectual traditions of the missionary, and because most of the evidence from this encounter comes from the missionary perspective, interpretations have tended to emphasize the role of the missionary. Two main viewpoints have emerged. One argues that the level of Native disorientation, demoralization, and dissatisfaction with old ways (due to an inability to cope with White society) determines the degree of acceptance of a missionary. The other holds that the leadership of the missionary is the key factor in the success or failure of a mission.

Those who hold the first view argue that Native people are incapable of dealing with the changes and problems posed by contact with European culture, and that the resulting insecurity renders their traditional patterns of living and thinking obsolete. Natives, it is said, can deal with Western ways during the first stages of contact because they can cope with any new problems by using traditional solutions. When contact intensifies, however, and more traditional ways are questioned, they feel the need for a new set of answers. At this stage, they often eagerly embrace the leadership of a missionary, who, they feel, will provide them with alternatives to their failing old way. The degree of Native acceptance of the missionary coincides with the level of dissatisfaction with old ways, and conversion is an attempt 'to restore their shaken self-confidence.'[1] As Judith Binney argues about early missionaries to New Zealand: 'The actual ideas of the religion itself did not make the people initially receptive to it.' Rather, the encroachment of White civilization, which took away their confidence to manage their own situation, drew them to the missionaries.[2]

Barnett asserts that the first Tsimshian converts to Christianity were those who had little prospect for social prestige or whose position in the community was not secure: namely, the older people, the disaffected, the orphans, the slaves, and the distant relatives of the leading families. For them, 'the acceptance of new patterns and standards [was] the means of relieving personal strain or dissatisfaction.'[3] In addition to the poor and the outcasts, Barnett notes that there were also chiefs among the converts who accepted Christianity because they saw it as a means for gaining new prestige. The cause of this disruption among the chiefs was the encroachment of Western ways, which spelled doom for the established social structure. In addition, liquor, firearms, and White diseases created strong feelings of despair and drew the Native people to the leadership of the Whites. The inability of old ways to cope with new problems, he concludes, spelled the end for traditional Native solutions.[4]

Morris Zaslow has accepted Barnett's position and claimed that the onslaught of Western civilization was simply too much for Native people. Tsimshian civilization was inherently weak:

> The sociologist would have detected serious weaknesses in their communal organization, the absence of any means for regulating intertribal wars and private feuds, for replacing savage caprice by the rule of law or of tempering the individual's struggle for personal success with some consciousness of the public good.[5]

The White world presented temptations and vices 'too fascinating for the Native in his present morally infantile condition to withstand.'[6] The demoralization produced by contact rendered Native people receptive to missionaries, and Duncan, concludes Zaslow, acted as a radical social reformer who gave them a new social order and environment – one that allowed them to gradually become self-assured people capable of functioning in White society.

Usher, on the other hand, has followed the second view and played down the role of Native demoralization. She, instead, has attributed Duncan's success at Metlakatla to his personality and leadership. The Tsimshian had avoided the cultural and physical breakdown of other tribes in British Columbia, and their long contact with White society had probably given them skill in integrating foreign elements into their culture. Thus, 'the European missionary ... may have found them exceptionally interested in new ideas and techniques, and well able to make use of them in their own lives.'[7] Nevertheless, 'Duncan's personality and the tactics he used in his work were the major reasons for his success in dealing with the Tsimshian.'[8] It was, she argues, his ability to compromise with and adapt to Native culture that attracted Native people and enabled him to establish a following. His leadership was responsible for the course of events at Metlakatla. Ironically, Usher herself has convincingly demonstrated that Duncan did not make concessions to Native ways, insisting rather on a total repudiation of old and a complete acceptance of new ways. Furthermore, as noted earlier, Usher's evidence does not do justice to the impact of contact and the effect of the annual migrations to Victoria.[9] The turning point for Duncan — the point at which he gained Tsimshian acceptance — was a demoralizing epidemic of smallpox. By rejecting demoralization, Usher has placed far too much emphasis on the role of leadership.

In his work on New Zealand missionaries, J.M.R. Owens follows the same framework as Usher but also attempts to deal with the problem of demoralization and cultural dislocation. He notes that cultural dislocation can often hinder rather than assist missionizing efforts. Disease, liquor, and firearms are often seen by Native people as harmful by-products of White civilization, and the missionary is frequently seen as part of these new problems.[10] Owens emphasizes missionary policy and tactics as determinants in the success or failure of a mission. The quality of the missionaries (e.g., whether or not they learn the Native language, and help to spread literacy, how they manage mission affairs, and the personalities of their leaders) is the crucial determinant.[11] Contact always produces some dislocation, but it is virtually impossible to decide when a culture is coping with change and when it is not. But, concludes Owens, however it is defined, cultural demoralization is not the primary factor leading to conversion and success in missions.[12]

On the surface, Crosby's personality and actions seem to fit the leadership model. As the *Methodist Recorder* reported:

> Mr. Crosby is a man of forcible presence and fine physique. He has great command of an audience, is a powerful and most impressive preacher ... He could not be long in a camp meeting and no one know of his presence, and somehow his spontaneous shouts of 'Amen' and 'Hallelujah' remind his younger brethren of that earlier type of Methodism.[13]

This kind of oratory and forcefulness appealed to the Tsimshian, who, Duncan reported, 'have a great idea of *strong* talk. Unless they feel affected at what is said to them, they regard the speech as weak.

If you can stare them out and speak loud, that is a strong speech.'[14] Crosby never backed down from any confrontation with what he regarded as evil. On one occasion he confronted a 'conjuror' who claimed he had more power than Crosby: 'It was then that the missionary felt it necessary to assume the role of the militant preacher; and, taking his position at the door, boldly challenged the savage to come on, at the same time suggesting what might be the consequences to him.'[15] Crosby was seen by his colleagues and the Tsimshian as a domineering, strong-willed individual, a man with intense convictions, full of energy and enthusiasm, and a spellbinding charisma.

There were other aspects of his personality that also appealed to the Tsimshian. As Gunson (in an exhaustive study of the missionary personality) has pointed out, in the early nineteenth century, missionary societies encouraged people of stamina and zeal, often unsuited for the home ministry, to work as missionaries.[16] The majority of these people were poorly educated, but they usually became more effective missionaries than did those with more education because they were often less timid in advancing new ways and eliminating the old. Many of them seemed to feel that they had to make up for their educational and social deficiencies by winning a large number of souls for Christ. They were usually tireless workers not afraid to put their hands to any task from felling trees to preaching the Word. Doubtless the Tsimshian admired someone who paddled his own canoe, built his own house, cut his own wood, and eagerly attacked any duty required by the immediate situation. They were impressed by someone who was unequivocal in his demands, had the personal authority to enforce them, and backed away from nothing.

In addition to this stamina and zeal, Crosby was not, as were many evangelical missionaries, hampered by self-doubt or captivated by Native culture.[17] He was periodically discouraged by Native responses to the gospel, but he never doubted the rightness of his task and did not seem to be afflicted by bouts of deep introspection and questioning. In fact, he attempted to create an environment which left little room for doubt or despondency. It is particularly significant that Emma Crosby was either 'sick,' 'worn out,' or doing 'badly' for most of her years at Port Simpson. Yet only once did Crosby allude to the nature of her illness. During the winter of 1885-6, he reported that Emma was having a difficult time recovering from the loss of two children to diphtheria. She was always 'in bed,' and this fact, combined with the lack of reference to a specific disease, seems to point to chronic depression. This conclusion is strengthened by the testimony of Agnes Knight, matron of the Girls' Home, who, reporting on the death of her father, wrote: 'I would give anything to have someone to talk to, one who would sympathize and cheer me, instead of being surprised that I feel sad and lonely – I wonder if they think the wound was only skin-deep.'[18] She indicates that Crosby seemed to have little patience for sadness or depression. Any questions or doubts that Emma may have had would have been treated with little understanding by Crosby.[19] Blistering hands, premature aging, aching bones, and fatigue inspired only such comments as 'it is glorious work to rescue the perishing and care for the dying.'[20] This duty outweighed personal feelings and doubts, and, for Crosby, was beyond question. The Tsimshian could never doubt the sincerity of his convictions.

As a poorly educated, lower-class immigrant, Crosby received much recognition and honour for his work. Missionary periodicals editorialized about his achievements at Port Simpson, and Crosby seemed to bask in the glory and honour it brought him. Even his autobiography contains numerous eulogies about his work. In the Foreword, the editors state:

> What deeds of heroism! What struggles and loneliness! What sacrifice of personal comfort and ambition! What inspiring faith and sublime hope! What determination, in spite of fearful odds! Enough here to make a romance that would stir the heroic heart of a nation with pride in the noble sons and daughters, willing to brave the hardship of isolation, and the dangers among savage tribes, that to those in darkness, they may bring the light of life.[21]

In 1893, the *Christian Guardian* published an article crediting Crosby with singlehandedly establishing all the missions, schools, and hospitals on the Northwest Coast.[22] Crosby's associate, A.E. Green, felt that the paper had gone too far and pointed out that the work in the area was the joint effort of all missionaries, teachers, and assistants, and that Port Simpson was Crosby's only true success. Even at Port Simpson, Crosby had not been the first missionary, and much of the heathenism had been removed before he got there. Crosby, Green added, 'is only one of its [Methodist Missionary Society] agents; and we could name others equally devoted, equally self-sacrificing, and equally successful in their work.'[23] Crosby published a letter in the paper a short time later pointing out that the original article had been misleading.[24]

Nevertheless, the prevailing opinion in Methodist circles was that Crosby had been responsible for making most of the dramatic changes at Port Simpson and on the Northwest Coast generally. As late as 1912, the *Western Methodist Recorder*, reporting on a lecture by Crosby, stated:

> We saw Port Simpson transformed under the power of the gospel from a village of semi-savages into a model community. We saw the Indian character unfolded in its weaknesses and strengths and caught the flame of the great revival which travelled so wondrously with Crosby and his workers from Simpson into the heart of Alaska and then we heard the lecturer declare with joyous tears that he would rather go back North with the gospel to 'those dear people,' than spend the next year in heaven.[25]

There is little doubt that Crosby could dramatically and effectively demonstrate how Port Simpson had been changed, and few Methodists doubted that Crosby had been God's instrument for this change. His personality easily led any audience, Tsimshian or White, to an emotional response.

Modern understanding of mission situations can easily be influenced by the dominance of a missionary personality and the literature describing his work. Indeed, missionary literature and travellers' accounts convinced observers that the Native people at Port Simpson had rejected their old ways and become 'Christian' and 'civilized'. To Crosby's contemporaries, this fact indicated that the mission was succeeding and that Crosby's leadership, with God's help, was responsible. Later analyses by Lockner and Greenaway do not eulogize Crosby's achievements as much as did his contemporaries. They have seen beyond the rhetoric which gave Crosby so much fame in his own days and have noted that Port Simpson was not the utopia Crosby said it was.[26] Nevertheless, they have adopted a similar line of understanding and Crosby's dominant personality has pervaded their analyses as well. They have defined the successes and failures of the mission in terms of Crosby's policies, blaming the tension of later years largely on Crosby's inability to move beyond primary evangelism. In the last analysis, the course of the mission is seen primarily as Crosby's responsibility. In a sense, they have been captivated by his spell-binding presence as well.[27]

The question remains: was it Crosby's leadership or Tsimshian demoralization which determined the course of events at Port Simpson? Both Greenaway and Lockner, while emphasizing Crosby's role, assume a certain degree of dislocation in Tsimshian society, enhancing the attractiveness of the option of Christianity. But dislocation is extremely difficult to define, and, while there were obvious negative consequences for the Tsimshian as a result of White contact, they did continue to use old patterns of thought and life long after their conversion to Christianity. It would seem that the reasons for their conversion and the subsequent course of events at the mission, while certainly influenced by negative elements of contact and by Crosby's leadership, are more complex than these positions argue.

Robin A. Fisher has attempted to bridge the either/or dichotomy between the roles of demoralization and leadership in his discussion of the Church Missionary Society missionary to New Zealand, Henry Williams. While Williams' leadership was responsible for bringing order and coherence to a previously mismanaged mission, Maori disorientation was probably as large a factor in making Christianity attractive as a new alternative. Yet, 'the answer to the question of what amount of change is necessary to enable the acceptance of Christianity, will in the final analysis be "whatever is present when a conversion occurs".'[28] In fact, different groups of Maoris were converted while in varying stages of cultural change. Cultural confusion, in some cases, led to a desire to restore old ways rather than to turn to Christianity. Furthermore, there were converts who never experienced dramatic social upheaval. The success of Williams's mission should thus be seen neither entirely in terms of changes in the Maori world nor in terms of missionary leadership. The leadership of Williams was crucial, but a new set of beliefs would not have been acceptable until the need existed, and such a need, concludes Fisher, often arises from new social forces.[29]

Fisher's analysis points to the difficulty of the leadership and/or demoralization views. He alerts us to the fact that there are two parties involved in the relationship, and while his conclusion seems to indicate that demoralization of some kind is necessary for conversion, he also points out that some people convert even though they are relatively secure in their traditional ways. It may be important to go beyond these standards for evaluating missions if we are to understand the dynamics of the missionary/Native relationship. Indeed, both views imply the inferiority of non-Western cultures and their inherent inability to cope with Western ways. The leadership hypothesis does this by implying that the missionary offers something which the Natives are unable to provide for themselves and which their society, by its very nature, lacks. A missionary's effectiveness, then, corresponds to his ability to provide Native people with the tools to cope with White contact. The demoralization view accepts this same basic premise, but maintains that the level of acceptance of a missionary is determined by the degree to which Native people have lost their orientation to life rather than by missionary policies. Thus both views implicitly maintain that Native cultures are inherently incapable of dealing with Western ways, and missionaries are evaluated in terms of how well the Native people in their charge deal with life in a Western context.

Both of these approaches, although not articulated in the same manner, are akin to the views of the missionaries, who went to foreign lands confident in the belief that they were coming from a *superior* culture to raise the standards of an *inferior* culture. As Max Warren has pointed out, however, the West's only superiority was technological – a superiority which had occurred because it had placed a premium on knowledge and the cultivation of reasoning power. But technological superiority was equated with moral superiority and was used to overpower other cultures. And he adds: 'It has been in terms of their irrationality that Western man, and not least Western missionaries, have dismissed the ideas which have shaped society in Asia and Africa.'[30] The missionaries to the Tsimshian were no different. They had not been trained in the study of other cultures and did not consider that these cultures could offer them anything of value.

Crosby was a typical representative of this attitude. He described Tsimshian religion as 'feeble and quite indefinite polytheism,' not 'a coherent system nor otherwise of a high order intellectually or morally.' He believed that they had only a vague notion of a supreme deity and worshipped anything that inspired awe.[31] The editor of the *Missionary Outlook* put it in stronger terms:

> It is surely the duty of the Church to seek the emancipation of the Indian mind from the slavery of ignorance ... He is a spirit self-hampered and suppressed. He has powers he cannot use and soul apartments he cannot occupy. Nature is to him an indecipherable scroll, a closed volume, a meaningless conundrum. To him the stars above are but dots of light and flowers beneath have for him no message and no meaning. How ignorance isolates the soul and shuts it up in a dungeon house.[32]

This ignorance, it was felt, was responsible for the Native peoples' inefficient economic practices, lack of individual enterprise to acquire wealth, neglect of mineral resources, and absence of adequate systems of communication. 'This apparent inability ... to dominate his environment provided perhaps the basic proof of backwardness.'[33] Backwardness was then equated with sinfulness.

Their view of the Native people led most nineteenth-century missionaries, whether Methodist, Anglican, or Catholic, to view them as children, needing the moral trusteeship of the White man. Native people, they believed, were dying off because their nomadic freedom could not compete with the coming of Western civilization. Furthermore, it was not conceivable that God would leave the wealthy lands of Canada in the hands of 'the wandering children of the forest.' As W.H. Withrow reported:

> We believe in every supplanting of a weaker by a stronger race to be a step towards a higher and nobler human development. But the right of conquest does not free from obligation to the conquered. We in Canada are in the positions of wardens to those weak and dying races ... We are their elder and stronger brethren, their natural protectors and guardians.[34]

Native people had to be treated tolerantly and patiently because they were 'just out of savagery.' They were seen as immature, childish products of poorly developed cultures, which, because they were not worthwhile achievements, had to give way to Western superiority.[35] Native people, reported many missionaries, were incapable of the rational thought (that is, abstract, Western philosophical and theological thought) and emotional experiences (such as Christian guilt and repentance) necessary for life in the modern world. They were similar to White children in that they needed training to acquire proper moral and religious insights.

Combined with this religious emphasis was the need to alter Native living arrangements. Tribal life hindered true civilization, which was built on individual opportunity and enterprise. Native people had to be encouraged, just as did any group of immigrants, to adopt the manners and styles of Canadians.[36] Education, manual training, and boarding schools would deprive Native people of their tribal roots, and 'the more intelligent the Native becomes the more he conforms to the habits of civilized life.'[37]

For propaganda purposes, missionary literature often made vivid contrasts between heathen ways and Christian ways. It was worth their while financially for missionaries to paint such contrasts, as the amount of support they could gain would often coincide with the immorality and degradation of the Natives as well as with the danger, adventure, and heroism demanded in changing them. Elijah versus Baal confrontations appealed to the sincere followers of mission work, as did the dramatic accounts of God's intervention (in an Old Testament manner) in aiding missionaries and their work and in casting judgment on Native wickedness.

While missionaries did embellish certain characteristics of Native life, they had little doubt about its childish and primitive nature. Agnes Knight, matron of the Girls' Home, reported that the girls asked such quaint questions as: 'Why did God make black men? How did White men get their skin White? I thought God didn't make Native people, He only made White people. Where do the stars come from, can you count them? Did you ever go to the country where Jesus lived? Were you on earth when Jesus came?'[38] Such responses to the gospel were expected and confirmed, for the missionary and his staff, the depth of Native ignorance. As Dennis Jennings reported: 'But still these Indians need nursing. They are as yet children. They must have all the which [sic] care, kind loving Christian hearts can give them – their former life having been so base. Peculiar tact is required to manage them, their prejudices and superstitions being welded into their very nature.'[39] There was surprise when the Native people showed an unexpected depth in their responses to Christianity. Jennings noted that: 'One asks why the Spirit of God comes into the heart and goes away again, and what we must do in order to have Him abide in the heart. They want to know the meaning of the Spirit's appearing in Christ as a dove.'[40] Such probings into Christian beliefs caught the missionaries off-guard.

Recent analyses of missions directed by early to mid-nineteenth-century Anglo-Saxon missionaries have generally not been as overt in their conclusions about the nature of Native cultures and the effects of European contact. While there are historians, such as Zaslow, who seem to have accepted, almost in its entirety, the missionary view of Native society, most offer perspectives which appear, on the surface, to reject the missionary bias but which, in effect, carry the same low opinion about the inherent capacities of Native societies to deal with Western ways of thinking, being, and doing. In a manner somewhat analogous to missionary attitudes there is, on the one hand, a deep regret that Native people were unceremoniously removed from a harmonious, ecologically sensitive way of life,[41] while on the other hand there is a recognition of a basic Native primitiveness and backwardness which inevitably had to succumb to the superiority of the West.[42] Virtually all historical literature on missionary/Native relations carries these assumptions, albeit in varying degrees and with varying emphases.

The analyses of the relationship between the Tsimshian and their missionaries follow this pattern as well. Usher, for example, has devoted an entire chapter to an examination of Tsimshian culture and has presented a picture of a well-ordered and integrated way of life. However, her view changes abruptly when she describes the effects of European contact. One major reason that the Tsimshian were not demoralized when Duncan first came to Port Simpson was that, 'being distant from White settlement, they were able to avoid the physical and cultural breakdown that befell the tribes near Victoria.'[43] When Duncan arrived, he proceeded to restructure Tsimshian society or, rather, to build a new structure in an isolated setting so that the Tsimshian would have a chance to acculturate without being swept away. Usher indicates that Duncan was successful, and she points to the numerous enterprises and policies which made Metlakatla a haven for Native people who, isolated from White settlement, were eventually able to survive in the new world. Duncan was thus responsible for saving the Tsimshian from the fate of the Native people living in Victoria. Usher does not spend a great deal of time examining how Native people felt about the situation or what struggles and emotions were involved in becoming Christian. She mentions only that many of Duncan's policies showed some continuity with indigenous practices and may have, thus, been palatable to the Native people.

The assumption about Native inability to cope with White ways and the neglect in examining their responses to missionaries arises because, as Freerk Ch. Kamma has pointed out, there has been

> a too facile tendency to suppose that the so-called primitive peoples are not capable either of discursive thought and reflection about their own cultural heritage or of adopting a critical attitude towards the great problems of life that will always exist, even with a relatively high degree of integration. The assumption appears to be that it is only through contact with Europeans that these people become conscious of their problems.[44]

He does not deny that contact with Europeans presented problems never before experienced, but he argues that Native peoples dealt with these by using, in large part, the same framework that they had always used.

The conversion experience perhaps best illustrates the complexity of Native response to European civilization. Analysis of early nineteenth-century South Pacific missions reveals a diversity of reasons for conversion. Some people were converted because they associated Christianity with material gain, others were confused about old ways, others enjoyed the novelty of the sacraments and ceremonies, some sought prestige in reading the Bible or using it to ward off evil spirits,[45] others enjoyed the emotional experience of revivals, some acceded to the persuasion or nagging of missionaries, others desired eternal life, feared hell, or sought immunity from disease, others made vows on the sickbed or during a dangerous experience, and, finally, some were converted as the result of a simple belief in the gospel as presented by their missionary.[46] Undoubtedly, for most converts, several of these motives operated at one time.

Reasons for conversion, however, must be clearly distinguished from the act of conversion. K.E. Read has pointed out that religious beliefs are not simply a logical set of ideas but are integrated into the life, the practices, and, indeed, the being of a people. They are more than a 'logically inter-connected system of ideas about the supernatural.'[47] They are part of a whole way of looking at the world and reflect an approach to life. While conversion is frequently seen as the replacement of one set of religious beliefs by another, it is in fact the acceptance of a whole new cultural framework. In the first chapter, a distinction was made between culture (the meaning system, values, ethos, and world-view of a people), social structure (the environment in which culture is made socially concrete), and religion (the 'network of symbols which give tangible expression to the orientation to life rooted in the cultural context.')[48] Conversion involves the adoption of a new cultural basis and thus includes a changed social structure as well as new religious symbols and experiences.

Missionaries frequently debated whether conversion to Christianity or the adoption of Western civilization should come first in the process of transforming Native cultures. They usually failed to realize the far-reaching effects of their mere presence among a culturally different people. There were many evangelical missionaries who placed an emphasis on salvation for the next world at the expense of life in the present one. But, as Kamma points out, all missionaries, even if they owned few possessions, brought with them, for their own comforts, products of Western culture which were foreign to the Native people. The Native people, more clearly than the missionaries, saw the horizontal ('in this world') as well as the vertical ('related to God') elements emphasized by the missionary teaching. The missionary was an incarnate gospel of the values attached to the Western way of life, even if he thought he was merely preaching 'the Word.'[49] For the Tsimshian, conversion was a deliberate and conscious attempt to embrace cultural forms which they believed would guarantee their participation in late nineteenth-century British Columbia society. Their reasons may have varied, from a desire for White goods to an admiration of Christianity, but, whatever the reason, conversion was a deliberate choice to substitute one culture for another, and not merely the substitution of new religious symbols and beliefs for old ones.[50] Inevitably, Native patterns of thought and behaviour remained after conversion, even though they may have thought that they had completely adopted a new way of life.

Their view of the Native people has prevented many students of missions from taking the conversion experience seriously. Because Native society and personality is seen as inherently weak, the Native role in conversion is largely neglected, and, instead, missionaries are often pictured as forceful and even domineering individuals who demand submission to their decrees. Indeed, many missionaries were powerful individuals, but often there is little appreciation for the fact that they would have been unable to carry out their programs had Native people not allowed them to do so. There are numerous examples in the history of missions where, after years of ceaseless toil, the missionaries had little return for all their efforts. Furthermore, the converts at Port Simpson did not include only disoriented Tsimshian who no longer had the ability to withstand the influences of White society or of powerful missionaries; their numbers included people from all levels of society with a wide variety of reasons for conversion.

The move to become Christian, with all of its horizontal and vertical dimensions, was a conscious, carefully considered decision. Barbeau's *The Downfall of Temlaham*, while perhaps over-romanticizing the Native past, nevertheless illustrates some of the complexity and soul-searching involved in the decision to become Christian – the difficulty in choosing between the familiar security, tradition, and wisdom of the old ways, and the prestige, social problems, and confusing morality of the Western way. There was little Native doubt concerning the complexity involved in the decision to convert.[51]

As noted in the first chapter, Native religious expression was integrated into the life of the people and symbolically expressed their cultural values. The 'great problems of life' were dealt with in a uniquely Tsimshian way. A sense of history and rootedness was established by a detailed knowledge of family origins and the maintenance of a rigid status system. Many ethical, judicial, and religious questions were dealt with in daily ritual and in the elaborate winter ceremonial complex, giving validity to such everyday activities as collecting food, building houses, and making clothes as well as setting standards and norms to enable the people to conduct themselves properly in all situations. Life maintained its meaning and integration according to the values that emerged from the rituals and ceremonies, and which were seen as inherent in the established order of the cosmos.

Thus, the Tsimshian at Port Simpson were aware of the difference between their traditional religion and culture and that of the Whites.

Throughout Crosby's first years at Port Simpson, they often made special reference to the fact that they had become Christian and had, further, embraced White civilization by constructing new houses, using different kinds of clothing, receiving education, and engaging in other activities similar to those practised by Whites. George Playtre has related a conversation with a Chippewa chief who refused to convert. The chief stated that

> when the Great Spirit made the White man and the Indian, he did not make them of one colour, and therefore did not design them to worship in the same way; for he placed the White man across the great waters, and there gave him his religion written in a book; he also made the White man to cultivate the earth and raise cattle, etc., but when the Great Spirit made the Indian, he placed him in this country and gave him his way of worship written in his heart, which has been handed down from one generation to another; for his subsistence, he gave him the wild beasts of the forests, the fowls that fly in the air, the fish that swim in the waters ... Now I suppose if the Great Spirit had intended the Indian to worship like the White man he would have made him White instead of red.[52]

The Port Simpson Tsimshian certainly realized that God's 'written' book and the White man's means of living contrasted to their traditional means of worship and living. However, unlike the Chippewa chief, this awareness was a contributing factor to their conversion. They decided that they wanted this other way of life, hoping it would be a better one. Conversion was a radically new orientation to life rather than the mere acceptance of new religious symbols and expressions.

The reasons for conversion at Port Simpson ranged, as Gunson and Fisher have noted of the South Pacific, from a desire for Western goods, the Christian God, and technology to a disillusionment with the seeming inability of the old ways to cope with such Western products as liquor, disease, and prostitution. Church membership records would seem to illustrate this range of motives. There was always a group which maintained its 'full membership' status, another that remained 'on trial' most of the time because of poor 'Christian habits,' while a third group fluctuated between 'full membership,' 'on trial,' or 'dropped'; support for the church coincided with the state of secular affairs at Port Simpson.[53] Demoralization or frustration with old ways was, thus, not in and of itself a precondition for conversion. It was merely one aspect of a problem posed by contact with an alien and technologically powerful culture. At Port

Simpson, the solution to this problem was a conscious choice by the Tsimshian to embrace what they interpreted to be the key elements of the success of Western culture. Cultural disruption was only one of a number of factors enhancing the attractiveness of Christianity as a new way of ordering life. The choice was not an easy one but was made in the hope that some of the alleged advantages of Western civilization would be theirs and that some of the negative effects of contact would disappear. There was the inevitable feeling of loss, but this was outweighed by what the Tsimshian hoped would be long-term benefits.[54]

It is also in this context that one must view leadership. Leadership in missions will only succeed if it meets the expectations of the converts and fulfils a need that they want fulfilled. Conversion only occurs because something offered has been found attractive, and, if the missionary successfully delivers what has been offered, his leadership will succeed. Leadership in and of itself, however, is not capable of making a mission successful.

At Port Simpson, Crosby was strikingly successful during his first years. His leadership was responsible for new houses, streets with lamps, a village council, and various bands and organizations. It seemed, to the Tsimshian, that their desire for participation in Canadian society was being fulfilled, and Crosby's leadership was as respected as it was effective. In later years, their prolonged absences from home, unemployment at Port Simpson, and frustration with the land question poignantly demonstrated to the Tsimshian that their hopes and dreams were not being realized. Frustration set in and Crosby's leadership lost its effectiveness. Because Crosby had not fulfilled their desire to be fully accepted by Canadian society, the Tsimshian decided to direct their own affairs and to find their own way to their goal.

Superficially, it would seem that the Tsimshian exploited Crosby to achieve their goals. However, the issue is not that simple. Exploitation implies deliberate manipulation and/or coercion. Crosby's ultimate goal to recreate the Tsimshian into model Christian, Canadian citizens paralleled their strong desire to embrace what they saw as central to White culture. Each party had reasons for wanting this relationship. Initially, these reasons coincided and resulted in a working relationship which satisfied both missionary and Native.

This does not mean that each party's understanding of acculturation was identical. The actual behaviour of Christian Natives often conflicted with what Crosby perceived to be acceptable Christian conduct. Crosby believed that conversion would automatically change the hearts and lives of the people and was distressed when his converts were still more 'Indian' than he wanted or expected them to be. But Crosby had no awareness of the complex processes at work when people steeped in centuries of one tradition suddenly convert to another. Missionaries such as Crosby did not make a deep examination of Native faith or religious practice and were seldom aware of 'how many different strands were woven into this religious behaviour.'[55] J.D.Y. Peel has posited that when Native people forsake their old ways for Christianity, what emerges is an entirely new product, neither the same as the old nor identical to the missionary view of Christianity. He disagrees with those who assume that all aspects of Native and European cultures are different and that these differences can be easily demonstrated. He believes that there are often elements in the old and the new that are similar in purpose and that it is extremely difficult to say which elements are pagan and which are Christian when a new syncretic form emerges.[56]

Crosby fits this explanation well. He did not realize that the new complex forms which emerged from his work were unique creations. John Webster Grant has noted that

> for the Indian the meaning of existence was already given, the purpose of religious practice ... being to maintain or restore equilibrium inherent in nature. Christianity calls for repentance from conformity to the present age and for commitment to participation in God's intended transformation of life. The Indian sought alignment with the cosmos so that it might remain in place.[57]

Human nature being what it is, similar practices may have entirely different meanings.

Geertz illustrates the complexity of cultural behaviour by using the analogy of a wink. The word 'wink' can be defined as the action performed when one rapidly contracts an eyelid. For one person a contraction is a nervous twitch, for another it is a conspiratorial act designed to give a deliberate message, for still another it is merely a rehearsal for a wink, and for yet someone else it is a parody of a wink.[58] Thus what Crosby saw in Native behaviour could easily have differed from what Native people were actually expressing, and what Native people saw in Christianity may also have been quite different from what Crosby was expressing. Spirit possession, prayer, and gift-giving were important elements of both Crosby's faith and Tsimshian religion. It was only in later years that Crosby began to realize that Native faith contained elements which were strictly Native in origin, even though in the context of worship they appeared to be Christian.

All of this does not detract from the fact that both Crosby and the Tsimshian had the eventual full participation of the latter in White culture as their goal. In his later years at Port Simpson, Crosby was burdened by a growing Native independence and desire to achieve, on their own, the participation in Canadian society that Crosby's leadership was failing to provide. This desire for independence was evident in their religious expressions as well. Crosby's realization, during these years, of the nature of Native faith made him reluctant to allow them this freedom. But he had little choice, and, despite his objections, the Tsimshian became more independent. Yet they never doubted the reality of their conversion. The establishment of the Band of Christian Workers and a brief affiliation with the Salvation Army clearly demonstrated that Tsimshian initiative and their movement away from missionary control was not a move away from Christianity and White culture.

It was not until the twentieth century, particularly after the First World War, that the Tsimshian realized that they would always be a group apart in Canadian society. Their initial frustration with the governments in the 1880s had caused them to lose faith in their missionary's ability to lead them into White civilization, but that goal remained. The twentieth century, however, is a record of the deterioration of this goal and of an increasing desire to return to traditional sources of meaning and ways of living. Missionaries, unwittingly, were largely responsible for unifying Native people in this quest to return to traditional cultural forms. During the time when many Native people suffered from the effects of alcohol, prostitution, and disease, the missionaries offered a viable alternative. Through the leadership of their missionaries, Native people regained some cohesiveness as a people, united in their resolve to worship the 'White God' and live as his 'civilized' people should. This unity enabled them to become aware of their close ties to each other as Native people, and when it became absolutely clear that they would remain the 'other' of Canadian society, this same sense of unity enabled them to attempt to reassert traditional values.[59]

In conclusion, it was neither Tsimshian demoralization nor Crosby's leadership that was ultimately responsible for the course of events at Port Simpson. In the early 1870s, there was a deliberate, conscious effort by the Tsimshian to change their cultural orientation by converting to Christianity, and they willingly submitted to Crosby's leadership. What he had to offer, and what they wanted, coincided. When circumstances deviated from what the Tsimshian felt conversion should entail, they turned from his leadership and attempted to complete the conversion process themselves.

Appendix

TABLE 1
Methodist Church of Canada

Year	Ministers	Members	Value of church property
1874*	1,031	101,946	
1878*	1,165	122,695	
1882*	1,192	125,420	
1883**	1,644	169,803	$ 6,809,817
1886	1,610	197,469	9,886,298
1890	1,748	233,868	11,597,491
1894	1,996	260,953	13,194,973
1898	2,031	280,537	13,473,381

* Wesleyan Methodist Church
** Methodist Church of Canada after union in 1883-4
SOURCE: Information from George Henry Cornish, *Cyclopedia of Methodism in Canada*, 2 vols. (Toronto: Methodist Book and Publishing House 1903)

TABLE 2
Methodist Missionary Society finances

Year	Income	Expenses
1875	$147,168	$185,268
1876	162,639	158,676
1877	145,998	174,255
1878	141,475	150,973
1879	135,223	140,090
1880	131,204	131,035
1881	134,842	137,078
1882	159,243	148,400
1883	159,228	169,652
1884	159,146	171,935
1885	180,129	202,042
1886	189,811	184,669
1887	201,874	189,286
1888	219,480	195,467
1889	215,175	210,691
1890	220,026	211,482
1891	243,015	219,980
1892	249,385	238,685
1893	224,778	231,983
1894	234,153	242,955
1895	237,496	238,286
1896	242,740	229,941

SOURCE: Information from Methodist Church of Canada, Missionary Society, *Annual Reports* (Toronto: Methodist Mission Rooms 1875-96)

TABLE 3
Statistics for the mission at Port Simpson

Year	Members On trial	Members Full	Baptisms Adult	Baptisms Infant	Sunday school Adult	Sunday school Total	Marriages	Abstinence pledge
1874	33	2					21	
1875	100	12	48	39			36	
1876	99	24					20	
1877	105	59					36	
1878	207	85						
1879	100	158	164*			210	30	
1880	190	117	151	165		680	49	
1881	240	167	46*			700	30	
1882	160	239				700		
1883	219	239			54	178		
1884	220	268			65	150		
1885	252	238	43	54	42	167	15	
1886	291	164	26	55	25	159	16	97
1887	314	171	21	32	0	110	6	108
1888	308	179	1	27	0	142	2	73
1889	106	248	1	24	0	148	11	
1890	116	241	12	33	0	106	11	
1891	149	185	0	33	0	150	8	128
1892	108	226	0	25	0	130	7	84
1893	154	233	30	29	20	174	22	150
1894	138	240	0	25			7	
1895	174	200	3	25	23	126	25	60
1896	186	200	0	21	23	107	4	5
1897	180	213	2	29	30	147	5	0
1898	180	213	0	16	30	142	8	125

* total for both adult and infant baptisms
SOURCE: Information in columns 2 and 3 from Methodist Church of Canada, *Minutes of Conferences* (Toronto: n.p., 1874-98). All other information from Methodist Church of Canada, British Columbia Conference, Port Simpson District, Minutes, 1883-97, and Thomas Crosby, Indian Work British Columbia, Handwritten Notes (1894?)

TABLE 4
School records

Year	Teacher	Students	Average attendance (daily)
1876	Thomas Crosby	106	
1877	C.S. Knott	122	42
1878	C.S. Knott	125	53
1879	C.S. Knott	119	50
1880	Susanna Lawrence	122	40
1881	Susanna Lawrence	86	32
1882	Susanna Lawrence	83	32
1883	Dennis Jennings	88	33
1884	George Hopkins	84	29
1885	Susanna Lawrence	82	35
1886	A.N. Miller	102	44
1887	A.N. Miller	96	42
1888	A.N. Miller	86	38
1889	R.B. Beavis	104	37
1890	R.J. Walker	71	29
1891	W.J. Stone	96	38
1892	S.W. Lazier	106	41
1893	Robert H. Cole	59	23
1894	Charles M. Richards*	66	19
1895	Charles M. Richards	73	26
1896	Charles M. Richards	94	23
1897	Charles M. Richards	85	27

* In 1895, a new school was opened which doubled as a boarding home for girls and was directed by Hannah M. Paul:

1895	32 girls	17
1896	25 girls	15
1897	32 girls	27

SOURCE: Information from Canada, Department of Indian Affairs, *Annual Reports* (Ottawa: Queen's Printer 1876-97)

Notes

ABBREVIATIONS

CMS	Church Missionary Society
CMSNP	Church Missionary Society, North Pacific Mission
DIA	Department of Indian Affairs
ERC	Ebenezer Robson Collection
GERC	G.E. Raley Collection
HBC	Hudson's Bay Company
PABC	Provincial Archives of British Columbia
RG10	Record Group 10
SGIA	Superintendent General of Indian Affairs
UBCIC	Union of British Columbia Indian Chiefs
UBCL	University of British Columbia Libraries
UCBCCA	United Church, British Columbia Conference Archives
UCCAT	United Church of Canada Archives, Toronto
WDP	William Duncan Papers

PREFACE

1 Lewis Hanke's account of an argument advanced by de Sepúlveda in *Aristotle and the American Indians* (Bloomington: Indiana University Press 1959), ix-x. Cited by Thomas Berger, 'Native History, Native Claims, and Self-Determination, *BC Studies* 57 (1983):11.
2 Henri and Mrs. H.A. Frankfort, 'Myth and Reality,' in Henri Frankfort, Mrs. H.A. Frankfort, John A. Wilson, and Thorkild Jacobsen, eds., *Before Philosophy* (Baltimore: Penguin 1971), 11-16.

CHAPTER 1: THE ORIGINAL PEOPLE

1 Margaret Blackman, 'Continuity and Change in Northwest Coast Ceremonialism: Introduction,' *Arctic Anthropology* 14 (1977):1.
2 C. Marius Barbeau, 'Review of Boas' Tsimshian Mythology,' *American Anthropologist* 19 (1917):548-63. Barbeau criticized Boas for using general myths rather than the less accessible but more valuable local and special ones. He was also critical of Henry Tate's (a Native) methods of acquiring information about the myths; Tate listened to Native people recite myths and later recorded what he heard, making it easy for him to forget, add to, or alter them. Barbeau's own research revealed discrepancies between Boas's work and the information given to him by Native people.
3 Marjorie Halpin, 'The Tsimshian Crest System: A Study Based on Museum Specimens and the Marius Barbeau and William Beynon Field Notes' (PhD dissertation, University of British Columbia 1975), 19-22.
4 Clifford Geertz, *The Interpretation of Cultures* (New York: Basic Books 1975), 144.
5 Ibid., 144-5.
6 Ibid., 142-69. Geertz describes such a conflict in Java, in which the social structure no longer expressed the cultural framework that still held meaning for many people.
7 Philip Drucker, *Cultures of the North Pacific Coast* (San Francisco: Chandler 1965), 124.
8 Ibid., 121-5, and Viola E. Garfield, *Tsimshian Clan and Society* (Seattle: University of Washington Press 1939), 20.
9 Wilson Duff, *The Indian History of British Columbia: Vol. 1, The Impact of the White Man*, Anthropology in British Columbia Memoir No. 5 (Victoria: Provincial Museum 1964), 102.
10 J. Daniel Vaughan, 'Tsimshian Potlatch and Society: Examining a Structural Analysis,' in Joy Miller and Carol M. Eastman, eds., *The Tsimshian and Their Neighbours of the North Pacific Coast* (Seattle: University of Washington Press 1984), 64.
11 Viola E. Garfield and Paul S. Wingert, *The Tsimshian Indians and Their Arts* (Seattle: University of Washington Press 1966), 35.
12 Ibid.
13 Garfield, *Tsimshian Clan and Society*.
14 Jean Usher, *William Duncan of Metlakatla: A Victorian Missionary in British Columbia*, National Museum of Man Publication of History, No. 5 (Ottawa: National Museum of Canada 1974), 31.
15 Drucker, *Cultures of the North Pacific Coast*, 40, and Philip Drucker, *Indians of the North West Coast* (Garden City: Natural History Press 1955), 124.

16 Duff, *The Indian History*, 102.
17 Drucker, *Cultures of the North Pacific Coast*, 50.
18 Garfield, *Tsimshian Clan and Society*, 216.
19 Drucker, *Cultures of the North Pacific Coast*, 55.
20 Irving Goldman, *The Mouth of Heaven: An Introduction to Kwakiutl Religious Thought* (New York: John Wiley 1975), 28.
21 Ibid., 49.
22 Marie-Françoise Guédon, 'An Introduction to Tsimshian World-View and Its Practitioners,' in Margaret Seguin, ed., *The Tsimshian: Images of the Past, Views for the Present* (Vancouver: UBC Press 1984), 144.
23 Margaret Seguin, ed., *The Tsimshian: Images of the Past, Views for the Present* (Vancouver: UBC Press, 1984), xiv.
24 Goldman, *The Mouth of Heaven*, 26.
25 Ibid.
26 Ibid., 139. On page 8, he notes that potlatches, 'even as they deal in "property" bind outsiders into formal exchanges, even as they reflect on the prestige of the chiefs, are basically and decidedly religious actions.'
27 *Handbook of North American Indians*, Vol. 7, William C. Sturtevant, ed. (Washington, DC: Smithsonian Institution 1990), 279, and Gisday Wa and Delgam Uukw, *The Spirit in the Land* (Gabriola: Reflections, n.d.), 23.
28 Goldman, *The Mouth of Heaven*, 8.
29 Gisday Wa and Delgam Uukw, *The Spirit in the Land*, 31.
30 Geertz, *The Interpretation of Cultures*, 89-90.
31 Goldman has failed to distinguish between culture and religion, identifying the cultural framework as religion rather than seeing religion as the expression of cultural values.
32 Garfield and Wingert, *The Tsimshian and Their Arts*, 50.
33 Mircea Eliade, *Myth and Reality*, World Perspectives, W.R. Trask, trans. (New York: Harper and Row 1963), 5-6.
34 Drucker, *Cultures of the North Pacific Coast*, 98.
35 Ibid.
36 Gisday Wa and Delgam Uukw, *The Spirit in the Land*, 36.
37 Stephen A. McNeary, 'Image and Illusion in Tsimshian Mythology,' in Joy Miller and Carol M. Eastman, eds., *The Tsimshian and Their Neighbours of the North Pacific Coast* (Seattle: University of Washington Press 1984), 3.
38 Ibid, 14.
39 Marjorie Halpin, 'The Structure of Tsimshian Totemism,' in Joy Miller and Carol M. Eastman, eds., *The Tsimshian and Their Neighbours of the North Pacific Coast* (Seattle: University of Washington Press 1984), 35.
40 See, for example, 'The Painted Goat of Skekyawden' in C. Marius Bar-

beau, *The Downfall of Temlaham* (Edmonton: Hurtig 1973), 223ff, and Calvin Martin, *Keepers of the Game* (Berkeley and Los Angeles: University of California Press 1978), Chaps. 1-4.

41 Garfield and Winger, *The Tsimshian and Their Arts*, 58, and Drucker, *Cultures of the North Pacific Coast*, 85. Drucker points out that the first salmon ceremony reminded the participants that the run was a voluntary sacrifice for the benefit of humanity, and when the bones were returned to the water during the ceremony, they were washed down to the sea, where, Native people believed, each fish would reassemble and return to life.

42 Halpin, 'The Tsimshian Crest System,' 10.

43 Goldman, *The Mouth of Heaven*, 3. Goldman adds: 'To give life to man, the animal must yield his own life.'

44 Seguin, ed., *The Tsimshian: Images of the Past, Views for the Present*, xiv.

45 Ibid., 117.

46 Katerina S. Reid, 'The Origins of the Tsetsega in the Baxus: A Study of Kwakiutl Prayers, Myth and Ritual' (PhD dissertation, University of British Columbia 1976), ii.

47 Ibid.

48 Ibid., iii.

49 Ibid., 187. See also Margaret Seguin, 'Let There be No Salmon: Symbols in Traditional Tsimshian Potlatch,' in *The Tsimshian: Images of the Past, Views for the Present*, 118.

50 Seguin, 'Let There Be No Salmon,' 111.

CHAPTER 2: THE ARRIVAL OF EUROPEANS

1 Drucker, *Cultures of the North Pacific Coast*, 117.

2 Jacinto Caamano, 'The Journal of Jacinto Caamano,' *British Columbia Historical Quarterly* 2 (1938):274-93. See also E. E. Rich, *The History of the Hudson's Bay Company, 1670-1870* (London: Hudson's Bay Company Record Society 1959), 2:626.

3 Drucker, *Cultures of the North West Coast*, 118.

4 Grumet, 'Changes in the Coast Tsimshian,' 305. He estimates that one-third of the residents of Port Simpson died. Sir George Simpson estimated that 500 died. See George Simpson, *Narrative of a Journey Round the World During the Years 1841 and 1842* (London: H. Colburn 1847), 1:207.

5 Robin Fisher, *Contact and Conflict: Indian-European Relations in British Columbia, 1774-1890* (Vancouver: University of British Columbia Press 1977), Chaps. 1 and 2.

6 William McNeill, in 1835, married a woman from the wolf phratry. This

marriage, along with Kennedy's marriage to an eagle, gave the Hudson's Bay Company a firm alliance with a significant portion of Coast Tsimshian society. Over the years, most of the Fort personnel married Native women.

7 John Work, *The Journal of John Work, January to October, 1835*, Archives of British Columbia, Memoir No. 10 (Victoria: King's Printer 1945), April 22, 1835.
8 John Work to John McLoughlin, February 26, 1844, Hudson's Bay Company, Fort Simpson, British Columbia, Correspondence Outward, September 1, 1841–October 11, 1844, signed by John Work, Provincial Archives of British Columbia (hereafter cited as PABC).
9 William H. McNeill, to Board of Management, August 26, 1852, Hudson's Bay Company, Port Simpson, British Columbia, Correspondence Outward, November 20, 1851–November 2, 1855, signed by Captain W.H. McNeill, PABC.
10 Work, *The Journal of John Work*, August 25, 1835.
11 Jean Usher, *William Duncan of Metlakatla*, 34.
12 Ibid., 38.
13 Fisher, *Contact and Conflict*, 47-8.
14 Drucker, *Cultures of the North Pacific Coast*, 190.
15 Work, *The Journal of John Work*, September 2, 1835. There are also numerous references to the middlemen role of the Tsimshian in the Fort Simpson Records for 1841-3.
16 Drucker, *Cultures of the North Pacific Coast*, 61-4.
17 Journal, Hudson's Bay Company, Fort Simpson, British Columbia, May 12, 1842–June 22, 1943, kept by John Work and Roderick Finlayson, March 23, 1843, PABC.
18 Ibid.
19 Reid, 'The Origins of the Tsetsega,' 189.
20 Calvin Martin, *Keepers of the Game*, 186-7.
21 Ibid., 59. Martin notes that most students of Native-European relations tend to analyze the fur-trading relationship in terms of western economic theory, particularly the laws of supply and demand, marketplace, and level of technology.
22 For details of Duncan's early life in England and of his Victorian framework, see Usher, *William Duncan of Metlakatla*, Chaps. 1 and 2.
23 Hamilton Moffatt to Dugald Mactavish, August 23, 1860, Hudson's Bay Company, Fort Simpson, British Columbia, Hamilton Moffatt Letterbook, 1859–April 9, 1861 and October 26, 1863–October 24, 1865, PABC.
24 Journal, Hudson's Bay Company, Fort Simpson, British Columbia, September 15, 1859–December 31, 1862, kept by Hamilton Moffatt and William H. McNeill, February 2, 1862. PABC.

25 Usher, *William Duncan of Metlakatla*, 50.
26 Ibid., 57-8.
27 Ibid., 52.
28 Journal, Hudson's Bay Company, Fort Simpson, British Columbia, September 15, 1859–December 31, 1862, kept by Hamilton Moffatt and William H. McNeill, July 5, 1862.
29 Usher, *William Duncan of Metlakatla*, 64.
30 The wealthy Legaic was one of the converts.
31 Usher, *William Duncan of Metlakatla*, 81.
32 Fisher, *Contact and Conflict*, 132.
33 Ibid., 133.
34 Usher, *William Duncan of Metlakatla*, 78. Usher is quoting Duncan.
35 Ibid., 82.

CHAPTER 3: REVIVALISM AND CIVILIZATION

1 *Methodist Recorder* 1 (1989):4.
2 William H. Withrow, ed., *The Native Races of North America* (Toronto: Methodist Mission House 1895), 193-4, and *Methodist Recorder* 1 (1989):4.
3 Thomas Crosby, *Among the An-ko-me-nums or Flathead Tribes of Indians of the Pacific Coast* (Toronto: William Briggs 1907), 24.
4 Ibid., 25.
5 Ibid., 24.
6 Ibid., 25.
7 Timothy Laurence Smith, *Revivalism and Social Reform* (New York: Abington Press 1957), 63.
8 Crosby, *Among the An-ko-me-nums*, 26. See also Neil Gunson, *Messengers of Grace: Evangelical Missionaries in the South Seas, 1797-1860* (New York: Oxford University Press 1978), 54-7. Gunson notes that it was a particular Wesleyan characteristic to see the direct hand of God in both conversion and everyday experiences.
9 Crosby, *Among the An-ko-me-nums*, 27.
10 William Taylor, *William Taylor of California, Bishop of Africa: An Autobiography* (London: Hodder and Stoughton 1897), 150 and 157.
11 Gunson, *Messengers of Grace*, 31ff.
12 Ibid., 59-60.
13 H. Alan C. Cairns, *Prelude to Imperialism: British Reactions to Central African Society, 1840-1890* (London: Routledge and Kegan Paul 1965), 19.
14 See, for example, *Centennial of Canadian Methodism* (Toronto: William Briggs 1891), 13ff.
15 Bernard Semmell, *The Methodist Revolution* (New York: Basic Books 1973), 17.

16 H. Richard Niebuhr, *The Social Sources of Denominationalism* (New York: World Publishing Company 1929), 67.
17 Maldwyn Edwards, *John Wesley and the Eighteenth Century, A Study of His Social and Political Influence* (London: George Allen and Unwin 1933), 182.
18 Wellman J. Warner, *The Wesleyan Movement in the Industrial Revolution* (London: Longmans 1930), 143, and Anthony Armstrong, *The Church of England, The Methodists and Society, 1700-1850* (London: University of London Press 1973), 92-3.
19 Warner, *The Wesleyan Movement*, 141, and Semmel, *The Methodist Revolution*, 73.
20 Warner, *The Wesleyan Movement*; Edwards, *John Wesley and the Eighteenth Century*; and Armstrong, *The Church of England* deal with this subject in more detail.
21 Kenneth E. Rowe, ed., *The Place of Wesley in the Christian Tradition* (Metuchen, NJ: Scarecrow Press 1976), 3.
22 William H. Elgee, *The Social Teachings of the Canadian Churches* (Toronto: Ryerson 1964), 82.
23 S.D. Clark, *Church and Sect in Canada* (Toronto: University of Toronto Press 1948), 152.
24 See, for example, Alexander Sutherland, *The Methodist Church and Missions in Canada* (Toronto: Department of Missionary Literature of the Methodist Church, n.d.), 85ff; George F. Playter, *History of Methodism in Canada* (Toronto: Wesleyan Conference Office 1862), 1:48ff; and A. Egerton Ryerson, *Canadian Methodism, Its Epochs and Characteristics* (Toronto: William Briggs 1882), 103.
25 Ryerson, *Canadian Methodism*, 104.
26 Virtually all American Methodist preachers left Canada during and after the War of 1812.
27 Ernest Richard Taylor, *Methodism and Politics, 1791-1851* (Cambridge: Cambridge University Press 1935). Taylor explains the conservatization of Methodism in England. Eventually, Canadian Methodists would follow the same pattern.
28 Goldwin French, *Parsons and Politics: The Role of the Wesleyan Methodists in Upper Canada and the Maritimes from 1780 to 1855* (Toronto: Ryerson 1962), 78.
29 Niebuhr, *The Social Sources of Denominationalism*, 54.
30 Clark, *Church and Sect in Canada*, 332.
31 The conservatism and shift from evangelical revivalism by the British Wesleyans in England led to divisions in two directions: Arminian liberalism, following the insights of the Enlightenment and Romantic eras, and old-style revivalism, ministering to the poor and working classes. In Canada, the union with the Wesleyans resulted in a similar

32 Clark, *Church and Sect in Canada*, 339.
33 Laurence S. Fallis, Jr., 'The Idea of Progress in the Province of Canada,' in W.L. Morton, ed., *The Shield of Achilles: Aspects of Canada in the Victorian Age* (Toronto: McClelland and Stewart 1968), 170-2.
34 Goldwin French, 'The People Called Methodists in Canada,' in J.W. Grant, ed., *The Churches and The Canadian Experience: A Faith and Order Study of the Christian Tradition* (Toronto: Ryerson 1963), 74.
35 Good examples of this are Crosby's missionary tours to Ontario in 1873-4, 1881-2, and 1989, which generated enthusiastic support.
36 Semmel, *The Methodist Revolution*, 144. In the context of the French revolution, the British Wesleyans had to prove their loyalty. They channelled their enthusiasm into missions as a matter of self-defence. For Canadian Methodists, no such danger existed. Nevertheless, their striving for respectability and acceptance also necessitated a different avenue for their Arminian enthusiasm. Missions fulfilled this need. See Semmel, 143-50.
37 William H. Brooks, 'Methodism in the Canadian West in the Nineteenth Century' (PhD dissertation, University of Manitoba 1972), viii; Erling G. Lindstrom, 'The Methodist Church, Canada, 1884-1912' (MA thesis, Simon Fraser University 1972), 7; and Gunson, *Messengers of Grace*, 47. Gunson notes about Wesleyan missionaries: 'They seemed to require constant renewals of the outpouring of the Holy Spirit. Revivalism came more frequently to the Wesleyan camp.'
38 Semmel, *The Methodist Revolution*, 148-9.
39 Crosby, *Among the An-ko-me-nums*, 38.
40 A feature also noted by Judith Binney, *The Legacy of Guilt: A Life of Thomas Kendall* (London: Oxford University Press 1968) and by G.E. Raley, Miscellaneous, Articles, Papers, etc., Relating to Indians and Missions, Raley Collection, PABC. Raley points out that Native people, before the coming of Europeans, were in a constant state of war concerning 'acquisition of territory rivalry of nations for chieftainship avenging of insult Jealousy revenge' [sic]. Victory, he notes, involved decapitation, slavery, scalp rocks, and cremations. Yet he admits that the 'happiest Indians lived beyond the advancing edges of civilization and order.' Native people had definite moral and ethical rules, were honest, and lived in 'utter devotion to truth among themselves until civilization destroyed their way of life.'
41 Crosby, *Among the An-ko-me-nums*, 55.
42 Ibid., 102.
43 Ibid., 105.

44 Ibid., 104.
45 Ibid., 62.
46 Ibid., 45.
47 Ibid., 49.
48 Ibid., 51.
49 Ibid., 178-9.
50 Thomas Crosby, *David Sallosalton* (Toronto: Department of Missionary Literature of the Methodist Church 1906), 26-7.
51 He wanted to go to college first and also see his parents but was persuaded not to because too many souls would be 'lost' in the meantime.
52 John MacLean, *Vanguards of Canada* (Toronto: Methodist Publishing House 1919), 192.
53 Crosby, *Among the An-ko-me-nums*, 143.
54 Ibid.
55 Ibid., 154.

CHAPTER 4: ACCULTURATION (RELIGIOUS LIFE)

1 C. Marius Barbeau and William Beynon, unpublished field notes selections from the Tsimshian file, compiled by Wilson Duff, in possession of the Museum of Anthropology, University of British Columbia, file 9, Gitands origins.
2 William Duncan to Church Missionary Society, February 24, 1874, Church Missionary Society, North Pacific Mission, Correspondence Inward (hereafter cited as CMSNP), microfilm, University of British Columbia Library (hereafter cited as UBCL) and William Beynon, 'The Tsimshian of Metlakatla, Alaska,' *American Anthropologist* 43 (1941):86. Beynon notes that Duncan expelled Dudoward because of his desire to become a 'cannibal Halait.'
3 Criminal charge, November 25, 1871, William Duncan, Civil Office, William Duncan Papers (hereafter cited as WDP), microfilm, UBCL.
4 W.H. Collison to Church Missionary Society (hereafter cited as CMS), January 10, 1874, CMSNP.
5 Duncan, Annual Report, January 29, 1874, CMSNP.
6 Duncan to CMS, February 24, 1874, CMSNP.
7 Duncan's point about Native collusion with the Hudson's Bay Company (hereafter cited as HBC) may have some degree of validity as the trader Charles Morison stated that they fully assisted the Methodists because Native people and the HBC saw very little of the CMS and 'for 13 years never heard the gospel.' See Charles Morison, 'Reminiscences of British Columbia from 1862,' typescript in possession of R. Geddes-Large, 67.
8 Duncan to CMS, March 16, 1874, CMSNP. He admitted that Pollard may

not have said this but, nevertheless, this was the message given to the people by the translators.
9 Duncan to CMS, February 12, 1875, CMSNP.
10 Duncan to CMS, March 16, 1874, CMSNP and Pollard letter, *Daily Colonist* (April 14, 1874).
11 Duncan to CMS, March 16, 1874, CMSNP. In February, twenty-two families left Fort Simpson for Metlakatla, according to Duncan. See also Duncan to Edward Hutchinson, CMS, April 8, 1874.
12 Collison to CMS, August 28, 1874, CMSNP.
13 *Daily Colonist* (April 14 and April 29, 1874).
14 Speeches by Matthew Johnston and Kate Dudoward, Grace United Church, Port Simpson, 'Banquet Speeches Commemorating the Arrival of Rev. Wm. Pollard, the First Ordained Minister to Visit Port Simpson, Feb. 22, 1934,' February 24, 1934, 1-4, United Church, British Columbia Conference Archives (hereafter cited as UCBCCA).
15 *Christian Guardian* (July 1, 1874) and Tomlinson to Duncan, June 28, 1874, William Duncan, Correspondence Inward, WDP.
16 Duncan to Crosby, November 16, 1874, William Duncan, Letterbooks, WDP.
17 Duncan to CMS, February 12, 1875, CMSNP.
18 Ibid.
19 Usher, *William Duncan of Metlakatla*, 96-7.
20 The passage reads as follows: 'And it shall come to pass afterward that I will pour out my spirit on all flesh; your sons and your daughters shall prophesy, your old men shall dream dreams, and your young men shall see visions. Even upon the menservants and maidservants, in those days, I will pour out my spirit.'
21 See Andrew Rettig, 'A Nativist Movement at Metlakatla Mission,' *BC Studies* 46 (1980):28-39. Rettig says that the spontaneity encouraged by Hall produced 'a spontaneous religious movement of mixed Christian and Native rites. What emerged, if only for a bierf [sic] moment, was a true synthesis of two religious traditions: the Tsimshian ritual of spirit visitation inlaid with Christian symbols'(39). A serious omission in this article is the lack of mention of the possible influence of friends and relatives at Fort Simpson, who, under Crosby, regularly participated in revivals.
22 J.W. Arctander, *The Apostle of Alaska* (New York: Fleming H. Revell 1909), 245.
23 Usher, *William Duncan of Metlakatla*, 96.
24 Hall to Duncan, February 1880, William Duncan, Correspondence Inward, WDP.
25 In 1880, the name was changed to Port Simpson. I will use this designation from here on.

26 C.M. Tate to elders of the Christian Church of Metlakatla, December 23, 1881, William Duncan, Correspondence Inward, WDP and Crosby letter, December 7, 1880, *Missionary Outlook* 1 (1881):60.
27 See Usher, *William Duncan of Metlakatla*, Chaps. 6 and 7.
28 Duncan to CMS, June 17, 1882, William Duncan, Correspondence Inward, WDP.
29 Crosby to Robson, September 10, 1887, Ebenezer Robson, Correspondence Inward, Ebenezer Robson Collection (hereafter cited as ERC), PABC.
30 C.M. Tate, 'Autosketch,' C.M. Tate file, UCBCCA.
31 Pollard letter, April 1875, *Missionary Notices* 3:56.
32 Crosby letter, February 16, 1876, *Missionary Notices* 8, 129, and Thomas Crosby, *Up and Down the North Pacific Coast by Canoe and Mission Ship* (Toronto: Missionary Society of the Methodist Church 1914), 56.
33 *Christian Guardian* (January 15, 1879), Crosby letter, December 18, 1884, *Missionary Outlook* 5 (1885):47, and Crosby to Robson, November 9, 1882, January 9, 1883, October 11, 1884, October 18, 1885, etc., ERC.
34 Crosby to Robson, October 18, 1885, ERC.
35 Crosby, *Up and Down the North Pacific Coast*, 47.
36 Ibid., 48.
37 Crosby report, Methodist Missionary Society, *Annual Report* (Toronto: Methodist Mission Rooms 1880-81), xiii. See also Crosby to Robson, January 9, 1881 (postscript, February 9, 1881), ERC.
38 Crosby letter, December 20, 1882, *Missionary Outlook* 3 (1883):75.
39 Crosby, *Up and Down the North Pacific Coast*, 55.
40 Green letter, April 5, 1890, *Missionary Outlook* 10 (1890):109.
41 Crosby report, Methodist Missionary Society, *Annual Report*, 1890-91, xxxi.
42 Crosby letter, June 23, 1891, *Missionary Outlook* 11 (1891):63.
43 Crosby to Robson, November 12, 1892, ERC.
44 Crosby letter, December 29, 1892, *Christian Guardian* (February 22, 1893).
45 Crosby, *Up and Down the North Pacific Coast*, 237-42.
46 Methodist Church of Canada, British Columbia Conference, Port Simpson District, Port Simpson Church Register, 1874-96, UCBCCA. Some other examples of members whose status constantly changed were Arthur Wellington, Herbert Wallace, and Matthew Johnston, to mention only a few.
47 Ibid. 1890 was a particularly bad year. Crosby reported: 'I had to drop many back on trial.' Leadership in the church was on the basis of the members' Christian commitment and not on social standing. There were chiefs among the leaders but not predominantly so. Crosby's requirement for church leaders was based on their faith.

48 Lockner, 'Nineteenth Century British Columbia Methodism,' 137-8, and Greenaway, 'The Challenge of Port Simpson,' 75.
49 Crosby letter, 1877, *Missionary Notices* 16, 273.
50 Crosby report, Methodist Missionary Society, *Annual Report*, 1880-1, xiv.
51 Crosby letter, April 30, 1989, *Missionary Outlook* 9 (1889):127. In 1883, Crosby reported that he had visited New Westminster and met some Port Simpson people who were working there at the time. He decried the availability of liquor and recommended that someone be appointed to minister to Native people at their summer jobs. See Crosby letter, August 8, 1883, *Missionary Outlook* 3 (1883):160.
52 Alexander Sutherland, 'Notes of a Tour Among the Missions of British Columbia,' *Missionary Outlook* 6 (1886):22.
53 Crosby, *Up and Down the North Pacific Coast*, 190-1.
54 H.G. Barnett, 'Applied Anthropology in 1860,' *Applied Anthropology* 1 (1942):24.
55 Crosby to Robson, March 8, 1888, ERC.
56 Crosby letter, n.d., *Home and School*, August 31, 1884, 142.
57 Alexander Sutherland, 'Notes of a Tour,' 2.
58 Jennings report, Methodist Missionary Society, *Annual Report*, 1888-9, xiii.
59 Green letter, April 5, 1890, *Missionary Outlook* 10 (1890):140.
60 Methodist Church of Canada, British Columbia Conference, Port Simpson District, Ministerial Sessions, 1889, 144, UCBCCA.
61 Ibid. (1892), 188.
62 Ibid.
63 Crosby to Robson, December 19, 1893 and January 13, 1894, ERC.
64 Methodist Church of Canada, British Columbia Conference, Port Simpson District, Ministerial Sessions, 1894, 221.
65 Henry Tate and Sam Bennett letter, n.d., *Missionary Outlook* 14 (1886):86.
66 Crosby to Raley, November 29, 1894, G.E. Raley, Correspondence Inward, Raley Collection (hereafter cited as GERC), PABC.
67 R. Geddes Large, *The Skeena, River of Destiny* (Vancouver: Mitchell Press 1957), 104.
68 Beynon, 'The Tsimshian of Metlakatla, Alaska,' 87. This was also noted by Crosby (see Crosby to Raley, January 7, 1895, GERC).
69 Osterhout to Robson, September 29, 1899, ERC.
70 Methodist Missionary Society, *Letter From the Methodist Missionary Society to the Superintendent-General of Indian Affairs Respecting British Columbia Troubles* (Toronto: n.p., 1889), 10, 24-9, 35, etc.
71 Ridley to Headquarters, June 16, 1888, CMSNP.
72 Ridley to Fenn, November 14, 1889, CMSNP.

73 Ridley to Fenn, June 17, 1890, CMSNP.
74 Ridley to Fenn, June 20, 1891, CMSNP.
75 Osterhout to Robson, December 7, 1898, ERC.
76 W.H. Collison, *In the Wake of the War Canoe* (Toronto: Musson 1916), 325-6.
77 Crosby to Robson, January 13, 1896, ERC. In addition to his duties as chairman of the Port Simpson district, Crosby had been appointed, in 1894, to be Superintendent of Indian Missions in British Columbia.
78 Crosby letter, November 1, 1876, *Missionary Notices* 11:180.
79 Crosby letter, July 4, 1877, *Christian Guardian* (September 12, 1877).
80 Crosby letter, June 5, 1878, *Missionary Notices* 18:312.
81 Acts 16:6-10. Paul had a vision of a man calling him to come to Macedonia to minister to his people.
82 Crosby to Robson, July 12, 1892, ERC.
83 Crosby to Raley, June 5, 1895, GERC.
84 Crosby letter, November 8, 1893, *Missionary Outlook* 14 (1894):6.
85 Crosby letter, August 24, 1880, *Missionary Outlook* 1 (1881):11.
86 Editorial, *Missionary Outlook* 2 (1882):18.
87 William H. Magney, *The Methodist Church and the National Gospel*, Bulletin 20, Committee on Archives (Toronto: United Church Publishing House 1968), 10.
88 See, for example, Rev. W.I. Shaw, *Methodist Magazine* 28 (1888):427-33. Shaw noted that 'when the world is in its best forms of development, it most prizes and studies these treasures of Greek and Roman thought and treasure.' In *Methodist Magazine* 40 (1894):397-404, Rev. A.H. Raynar argued for the need to combine the best of Greek and Christian worlds, and cites Paul as an example of such a combination.
89 S.D. Clark, *Church and Sect in Canada*, 400. Clark points out that revivalism attracted the poor, while the large churches, of which the Methodists were so proud, attracted the rich. Methodism addressed its appeal to those with wealth and status, and carefully channelled revivalism through such agencies which used professional evangelists.
90 Erling G. Lindstrom, 'The Methodist Church, Canada, 1884-1912' (MA thesis, Simon Fraser University 1972), 29ff.
91 Magney, *The Methodist Church*, Chaps. 1 and 2.
92 Ibid., 33. This development led directly to the social gospel movement at the turn of the century. See also the indexes of the *Methodist Magazine* after 1894.
93 *Christian Guardian* (February 22, 1882).
94 Editorial, *Missionary Outlook* 5 (1885):148. The editor estimated that one penny per day per member would raise $670,000 annually. This estimate, in 1885, was more than twice the actual budget (see Table 2 in Appendix).

95 See Tables 1 and 2 in Appendix.
96 Editorial, *Home and School*, February 9, 1889.
97 John Webster Grant, *The Church in the Canadian Era* (Toronto, Montreal: McGraw-Hill Ryerson 1972), 47.
98 Crosby report, Methodist Missionary Society, *Annual Report*, 1876-7, xii.
99 Crosby to Robson, September 10, 1887, ERC.
100 Sutherland to Crosby, September 25, 1889, Methodist Church of Canada, Missionary Society, Letterbooks, 175, United Church of Canada Archives (hereafter cited as UCCAT). See also Crosby, *Up and Down the North Pacific Coast*, 85. Crosby recalled an instance in which he filled a mission without notifying Toronto: 'There was no time to send work to Toronto or to wait 12 or 13 months until the Mission Board should sit, to find out whether they could have a missionary or not.'
101 Sutherland to Crosby, October 16, 1889, Methodist Church of Canada, Missionary Society, Letterbooks, 227, UCCAT.
102 Ibid., 226.
103 Sutherland to Crosby, February 16, 1897, Methodist Church of Canada, Missionary Society, Letterbooks, n.p.
104 Sutherland to Crosby, October 17, 1895, Methodist Church of Canada, Missionary Society, Letterbooks, n.p.

CHAPTER 5: ACCULTURATION (SECULAR LIFE)

1 Usher, *William Duncan of Metlakatla*, 11-28. Such beliefs were common to most Anglo-Saxon people in the nineteenth century. Although missionaries were often many years behind the latest ideologies and doctrines (see last chapter), they did adhere to the belief about the relationship between Christianity and civilization.
2 J.E. MacMillan to Alfred and Kate Dudoward, October 30, 1873, Letter, UCBCCA.
3 Crosby, *Up and Down the North Pacific Coast*, 83.
4 Ibid., 73.
5 Pollard to Powell, August 19, 1876, Canada, Department of Indian Affairs, Black Series, Western Canada, Record Group 10 (hereafter cited as RG10), vol. 3612, file 3878, Union of British Columbia Indian Chiefs Library (hereafter cited as UBCIC).
6 The only exception was from 1886-8, when A.N. Miller was the teacher.
7 Methodist Church of Canada, British Columbia Conference, Port Simpson District, Ministerial Sessions, 1893, 188.
8 Kate Hendry to home, December 26, 1882, Kate Hendry, Letterbook, PABC.

9 Kate Hendry to her sister, July 11, 1883, Kate Hendry, Letterbook.
10 Emma Crosby letter, *Missionary Outlook* 1 (1881):141.
11 Thomas Crosby letter, *Missionary Outlook* 9 (1889):100. Parents who boarded their children had to pay for the costs of maintenance.
12 A.E. Bolton letter, *Onward*, April 25, 1891, 133.
13 Shaw to Bolton, September 28, 1889, A.E. Bolton, Correspondence Inward, Bolton Collection, PABC. Shaw reported that the Methodist Missionary Society could not undertake financial support for such a venture: 'I have my fears as to the financial sweep of a physician in that region of country not because one is not needed badly enough, but on account of the circumstances of the people.'
14 Crosby, *Up and Down the North Pacific Coast*, 302.
15 Ibid., 80.
16 Elizabeth E. Long and Thomas Crosby, *How the Light Came to Kitamaat* (Toronto: Woman's Missionary Society 1907), 15.
17 Crosby, *Up and Down the North Pacific Coast*, 74.
18 Powell report, Canada, Department of Indian Affairs (hereafter cited as DIA), *Annual Report* (Ottawa: Queen's Printer 1879), 119.
19 Crosby letter, October 22, 1878, *Christian Guardian* (January 15, 1879).
20 Crosby letter, September 5, 1875 (*Christian Guardian*, November 4, 1875).
21 Crosby, *Up and Down the North Pacific Coast*, 313-15.
22 Crosby letter, February 16, 1876, *Missionary Notices* 8, 130.
23 Crosby, *Up and Down the North Pacific Coast*, 65.
24 Ibid., 66.
25 Chiefs and leading men of Tsimshian tribes to the Superintendent-General of Indian Affairs (hereafter cited as SGIA), October 3, 1878 (penned by Crosby), RG10, vol. 3668, file 10619.
26 H.G. Barnett, 'Invention and Cultural Change,' *American Anthropologist* 44 (1942):24-5.
27 Garfield, *Tsimshian Clan and Society*, 224-6.
28 Ibid., 280-1.
29 Ibid., 228.
30 Ibid., 240-55.
31 Crosby, *Up and Down the North Pacific Coast*, 310-11.
32 Ibid., 71-2.
33 Crosby letter, *Home and School*, March 14, 1885, 43.
34 Kate Hendry to her friends, January 21, 1884, Kate Hendry Letterbooks. During the festive season of 1883, reported Kate Hendry, Kate Dudoward gave a party at which there were noisy speeches and plays. The women were painted and wore skin blankets while they re-enacted some of their old performances 'which were both noisy and ridiculous.

I could not say anything against them as they had said they done [sic] it to let me see what they used to do before they heard the gospel.' On New Year's Day another such feast occurred.
35 Sutherland, 'Notes of a Tour,' 3.
36 Ibid., 22.
37 Ibid. Crosby was not blamed for his absences. The Tsimshian, in fact, asked Sutherland to send help for Crosby, obviously not aware of the relationship between the two. Thomas Wright noted that Crosby's workload was too great; he 'is nearly worn out with hard work.'
38 Ibid., 3. Crosby, in the *Home and School*, March 14, 1885, reported that 'they are away from home so much that it is very much against advancement among them.' He never considered that his demands for a different lifestyle created the need for their travelling nor that the Tsimshian were expecting him to remain at home to teach them new skills so that travel could be eliminated.
39 William Beynon, 'The Tsimshian of Metlakatla, Alaska,' 87. Beynon was critical of Crosby for not developing industry at Port Simpson but instead keeping the Tsimshian dependent upon seasonal employment and hindering their educational progress and continuity. In 1894, Crosby met Tomlinson (ex-Church Missionary Society missionary who had left the Anglican Church at the same time as Duncan) who had built a self-sufficient community on the model of Metlakatla. Crosby's travelling and perhaps the nature of his gospel kept him from undertaking such ventures.
40 For details of the federal and provincial governments' handling of this problem, see Robin Fisher, *Contact and Conflict*, Chap. 8, and Robert E. Cail, *Land, Man and the Law: The Disposal of Crown Lands in British Columbia, 1871-1913* (Vancouver: University of British Columbia Press 1974).
41 Fisher, *Contact and Conflict*, 188.
42 Methodist Missionary Society, *Letter From the Methodist Missionary Society*, v.
43 Crosby letter, January 20, 1875, *Missionary Notices* 2, 38.
44 Crosby letter, February 16, 1876, *Missionary Notices* 8, 130, and Crosby report, Methodist Missionary Society, *Annual Report*, 1875-6, xii.
45 A.E. Green, November 27, 1888, Methodist Missionary Society, *Letter from the Methodist Missionary Society*, 14-20.
46 Molyneux St. John, *The Sea of Mountains, An Account of Lord Dufferin's Tour Through British Columbia in 1876*, 2 vols. (London: Hurst and Blackett 1877), 1:321-2.
47 Ibid., vol. 2, 223-4.
48 Indian Superintendent I.W. Powell's report, Canada, DIA, *Annual Report*, 1879, 121.

49 Crosby to Powell, August 16, 1879 and Powell to Crosby, September 6, 1879 (copies of letters), British Columbia, *Papers Relating to the Commission Appointed to Enquire into the State and Condition of the Indians of the North-West Coast of British Columbia* (Victoria: R. Wolfenden 1888), 462B.
50 O'Reilly to SGIA (copy of letter), April 8, 1882, Canada, DIA, *Annual Report*, 1882, 90.
51 O'Reilly to SGIA, October 25, 1882, RG10, vol. 3605, file 2806.
52 Crosby to SGIA, June 28, 1882, RG10, vol. 3605, file 2806.
53 Powell to SGIA, August 28, 1882, RG10, vol. 3605, file 2806.
54 Such implicit acceptance of the notion of Native right to title was also noted by Rev. Tomlinson in 1884: see British Columbia, *Return to an Order ... for all Correspondence Relating to the Recent Indian Troubles on the North-West* (Victoria: R. Wolfenden 1885), 277-8, and 283. In a letter to John Robson, February 7, 1884, Tomlinson pointed out how Native people, from time immemorial, had held exclusive rights to property and prosecuted trespassers. Recently, he added, two cases of trespass, by Native people, on other Native peoples' territory were tried by justices MacKay and Duncan. The Attorney General of British Columbia had upheld both decisions, thus acknowledging Native rights to their hunting and fishing territories. But O'Reilly had curtailed any rights to property beyond the reserve and the Native people were upset because their hereditary rights to certain properties were being violated. Robson replied to Tomlinson on February 29 that the government would not disturb any Native hunting or fruit-gathering areas 'at least until such time as the lands are required.' Trespass, however, was a domestic dispute, and a justice of the peace could not enforce laws on trespass. On October 20, 1884, Tomlinson informed Robson that the Native people were most upset at the arbitrariness implied in the use of the word 'required.'
55 *Daily Colonist* (May 8, 1883).
56 Ibid. (May 10, 1883).
57 Methodist Missionary Society, *Letter from the Methodist Missionary Society*, 49.
58 Report of Meeting of Port Simpson Indians with MacKay, December 8, 1883, RG10, vol. 3605, file 2806. Powell emphatically denied this charge. See Powell to SGIA, January 9, 1884, RG10, vol. 3818, file 57837.
59 *Daily Colonist* (November 1, 1883).
60 Testimony of Arthur Wellington, Report of Meeting of Port Simpson Indians with MacKay, December 8, 1883, RG10, vol. 3605, file 2806.
61 Ibid.
62 MacKay to Powell, December 24, 1883, RG10, vol. 3818, file 57837.
63 Usher, *William Duncan of Metlakatla*, 128.
64 British Columbia, *Metlakatla Inquiry, 1884, Report of the Commissioners*

Together with the Evidence (Victoria: R. Wolfenden 1885), 134.
65 Ibid., Evidence, iv.
66 Crosby to John Robson, October 6, 1886, John Robson, Correspondence Inward, John Robson Collection, PABC.
67 For details, see Usher, *William Duncan of Metlakatla*, Chap. 7.
68 Statement of Crosby, Methodist Missionary Society, *Letter from the Methodist Missionary Society*, 4. See also Native testimony in British Columbia, *Papers Relating to the Commission*, 447.
69 British Columbia, *Report of Conferences Between the Provincial Government and Indian Delegates from Fort Simpson and Naas River* (Victoria: R. Wolfenden 1887), 253. See also Memorandum, Deputy SGIA Vankoughnet to SGIA, July 3, 1889, RG10, vol. 3818, file 57837. Vankoughnet noted that the missionaries 'do not give the Indians', but their own version of the matters brought before him [Powell] and occasionally more was said than the Indians knew of or intended.'
70 British Columbia, *Report of Conferences*, 255.
71 Ibid., 256.
72 Ibid., 260.
73 Crosby to Ebenezer Robson, February 9, 1887, ERC.
74 SGIA to Privy Council, May 27, 1887, Canada, DIA, Deputy Superintendent-General's Letterbooks, 61, UBCIC.
75 British Columbia, *Papers Relating to the Commission*, 416.
76 Ibid., 449.
77 David Leask on behalf of the Port Simpson Council to MacKay, November 30, 1883, RG10, vol. 3818, file 57837.
78 British Columbia, *Papers Relating to the Commission*, 425.
79 Ibid.
80 Ibid., Special Appendix No. 2, cvii.
81 Port Simpson Chiefs to Todd, January 5, 1888, RG10, vol. 3776, file 37373-2.
82 Metlakatla and Kincolith accepted the Indian Advancement Act in 1888.
83 Cornwall to SGIA, December 8, 1887, RG10, vol. 3776, file 37373-2. Todd accused the missionaries of controlling the village councils by punishing lawbreakers who did not follow 'their own interpretations of the laws of Moses.' See Todd report, Canada, DIA, *Annual Report*, 1889, 202.
84 Cornwall to SGIA, December 8, 1887, RG10, vol. 3776, file 37373-2.
85 *Daily Colonist* (May 17, 1888).
86 Ibid. (May 28, 1888).
87 Todd to Powell, June 12, 1888, RG10, vol. 3776, file 37373-2.
88 Jennings to Robson, January 15 and February 17, 1889, ERC.
89 Vankoughnet to SGIA, October 17, 1888, Canada, DIA, Deputy Superintendent-General's Letterbooks, 546-8.
90 The only exception was Ebenezer Robson, whose brother John held var-

ious positions in the government over the years. On November 14, 1888, Robson sent Crosby a letter in which he expressed extreme displeasure over a recent speech of Crosby's which was 'insulting to my own brother.' Crosby's actions could only serve to embarrass the Methodist position with respect to the government. In 1888, the British Columbia Conference of the Methodist Church appointed a memorial committee, with Robson as chairman, to analyze the 'Indian question,' especially Native/government relations. The 1889 Port Simpson Ministerial Session expressed regret 'that all reference to the land Question, the essential point at Stake and the foundation of the whole grievance ... was eliminated from the Memorial.' See Methodist Church of Canada, British Columbia Conference, Port Simpson District, Ministerial Sessions, 1889, 117. Robson was subsequently dropped from the committee appointed to discuss the Native question with Dewdney in the summer of 1889. See Robson to Crosby, November 14, 1888, Ebenezer Robson, Letterbook, ERC.

91 Methodist Church of Canada, British Columbia Conference, *Minutes* (Toronto: n.p., 1888), 28-9.

92 The matters reviewed were early Native fears over their land, Powell's unfulfilled promises, O'Reilly's surveys despite Tsimshian protest, MacKay's failure to answer their demands, the 'land grab,' HBC claims, their refusal to accept the Indian Advancement Act or an agent, the abolition of their village council and loss of legal power, the grant of traditional sites to the Anglican Kincolith Natives, the refusal of the government to allow missionary interpreters, the surveyors who came before the 1887 commission, the behaviour of the commission, and the division of the reserve and granting of an industrial school to Ridley's Metlakatla.

93 Statement of Chief Herbert Wallace, Methodist Missionary Society, *Letter From the Methodist Missionary Society*, 57.

94 Letter of Port Simpson chiefs and others in reply to Commissioner Cornwall's speech at close of Port Simpson meeting (not included in the Commission's report), October 24, 1887, Methodist Missionary Society, *Letter from the Methodist Missionary Society*, 42.

95 Affidavit of Arthur Wellington Clah, December 8, 1888, Methodist Missionary Society, *Letter From the Methodist Missionary Society*, 43-4. The reference to Ahab and Naboth can be found in I Kings 21:1-16, in which Ahab coveted a vineyard belonging to Naboth. Naboth refused to sell land which had been his family's traditional site for years, so Ahab's wife, Jezebel, arranged to have Naboth falsely tried for treason and executed. Ahab then took possession of the land.

96 Sutherland to Crosby, October 16, 1889, Methodist Church of Canada, Missionary Society, Letterbooks, 226.

97 Methodist Church of Canada, British Columbia Conference, Port Simpson District, Ministerial Sessions, 1891, 151.
98 Memorandum, Vankoughnet to SGIA, July 3, 1889, RG10, vol. 3818, file 57837.
99 Ibid. In June of 1891, Vankoughnet expressed delight at the fact that Crosby was to leave Port Simpson and he hoped that a more judicious man would replace him, 'as he caused, and, I think, always would cause division.' But on July 6 he expressed regret that his information had been incorrect. He added: 'Influence will be brought to bear upon church authorities to send some person who will work harmoniously with the Department. This, of course, is strictly for yourself.' See Vankoughnet to Vowell, June 11, 1891 and July 6, 1891, Canada, DIA, Deputy Superintedent-General's Letterbooks, 460 and 694. Earlier in April he had approved a grant for the Girls' Home. He had not wanted to but he felt the problems at Port Simpson were not the fault of the Tsimshian and that they should not be penalized for missionary behaviour. See Vankoughnet to SGIA, April 24, 1891, RG10, vol. 3853, file 77025.
100 Todd report, August 26, 1889, Canada, DIA, *Annual Report*, 1889, 119.
101 Residents of Port Simpson to Hall, June 8, 1891, RG10, vol. 3852, file 76586.
102 Ibid.
103 Hall to Vowell, March 9, 1891, RG10, vol. 3852, file 76586.
104 Vankoughnet to Vowell, April 28, 1891, RG10, vol. 3852, file 76586.
105 Memorandum, Ebenezer Robson to John Robson, April 29, 1889, John Robson, Correspondence Inward, John Robson Collection.
106 A.E. Green letter, February 19, 1890, *Missionary Outlook* 10 (1890):93.
107 Todd reports, August 26, 1889 and July 12, 1894, Canada, DIA, *Annual Reports*, 1889, 188, and 1894, 163.
108 Todd report, July 12, 1894, Canada, DIA, *Annual Report*, 1894, 163. Contrast this to Fisher, *Contact and Conflict*, 211, in which he states that by the late 1880s, '"the great potlatch" was not one to which the Indians would be invited.' For the Port Simpson Native, at least, this was not true.
109 Chiefs of Port Simpson to Todd, November 1893, RG10, vol. 3862, file 83121.
110 Chiefs and Council of Port Simpson to Vowell, January 30, 1897, RG10, vol. 3853, file 78547.
111 Chiefs of Port Simpson to SGIA, January [?], 1897, GER.
112 Todd to Vowell, March 23, 1897, RG10, vol. 3853, file 78547.
113 'We the Indians of Port Simpson and we all belong to the Salvation Army' to Todd, n.d., RG10, vol. 3853, file 78547. This group expressed support for the job Todd was doing at Port Simpson and wanted him to remain. They called him a just leader, unlike Crosby, who did not dis-

courage the Methodists and Band of Christian Workers from bullying their people. There were no chiefs who signed this list. This whole affair underscores how serious the tension was between the different religious groups vying for power.
114 Robson diary, October 28, 1897, Ebenezer Robson, Diaries, 1897-8, ERC. One of the government's quickest decisions concerned the dispute with the HBC, which was resolved in 1929, when the HBC was persuaded to convey the land in question to the Native people.
115 Todd report, Canada, DIA, *Annual Report*, 1897, 87. Todd made no mention of his troubles at Port Simpson. Indian agent reports at this time became statistical and formalized, making them poor sources of information.
116 James Woodsworth, *Thirty Years in the Canadian Northwest* (Toronto: McClelland and Stewart 1917), 194.
117 Ibid., 192. A.E. Green, in the mid-1880s, much to Crosby's consternation, became a missionary trader and built a cannery a few years later. In these ventures, he passed the profits back to the Native people, much as Duncan had done to make his people self-sufficient. In 1897, Green left the Methodist Church.
118 Rolf Knight, *Indians at Work*, 17-27.
119 These plans never came to fruition, as Prince Rupert became the new port when the HBC refused to sell their harbour property for the price offered by the government.
120 Sutherland to Crosby, March 9, 1895, Methodist Church of Canada, Missionary Society, Letterbooks, 952.
121 Sutherland to Matthew Johnston, March 9, 1895, Methodist Church of Canada, Missionary Society, Letterbooks, 944.
122 Crosby to Robson, January 13, 1896, ERC.
123 Robson Diary, June 30, 1987, Ebenezer Robson, Diaries, 1897-8, ERC.

CHAPTER 6: ROLE OF THE TSIMSHIAN IN CONVERSION

1 Harrison M. Wright, *New Zealand, 1796-1840, Early Years of Western Contact* (Cambridge, MA: Harvard University Press 1959), 183.
2 Judith Binney, 'Christianity and the Maoris to 1840: A Comment,' *New Zealand Journal of History* 3 (1969):165. See also Fisher, *Contact and Conflict*, Chaps. 1 and 2, where the point is made that Native people reacted to White contact during the fur-trade period by using traditional means.
3 Barnett, 'Personal Conficts,' 167, and Barnett, 'Applied Anthropology in 1860,' 21-2.
4 Barnett, 'Personal Conficts,' 168-71.
5 Morris Zaslow, 'The Missionary as Social Reformer: The Case of Wil-

liam Duncan,' *Journal of the Canadian Church Historical Society* 8 (1966):54.
6 Ibid., 60.
7 Usher, *William Duncan of Metlakatla*, 52.
8 Ibid.
9 See page 22, this book.
10 J.M.R. Owens, 'Christianity and the Maoris till 1840,' *New Zealand Journal of History* 2 (1968):24.
11 Ibid., 33-4.
12 Niel Gunson, *Australian Reminiscences and Papers of L.E. Threlkeld*, Australian Aboriginal Studies No. 40, Ethnohistory Series No. 2 (Canberra: Australian Institute of Aboriginal Studies, n.d.), 9. Gunson points out that the Australian aborigines did not convert, even though evidence suggests that they were demoralized by the effects of White contact, a condition usually accepted as the reason for conversion.
13 *Methodist Recorder* 1 (1899):4.
14 Usher, *William Duncan of Metlakatla*, quoting Duncan Journal, June 8, 1859, 53.
15 Crosby, *Up and Down the North Pacific Coast*, 255.
16 Gunson, *Messengers of Grace*, 86 and 97.
17 He was quite similar to Henry Williams of New Zealand whose leadership was powerful, forthright and unequivocal, and unhampered by self-doubt. See Robin A. Fisher, 'Henry Williams' Leadership of the Church Missionary Society Mission in New Zealand, 1823-1840' (MA thesis, University of Auckland 1969), 72. Thomas Kendall, on the other hand, was fascinated by certain characteristics of Native culture and, in the end, was swallowed up by his guilt about this fascination. See Judith Binnery, *The Legacy of Guilt: A Life of Thomas Kendall* (London: Oxford University Press 1968).
18 Agnes Walker (Knight), Journal, October 5, 1886, PABC.
19 Susanna Lawrence was closer to Crosby's ideal. In a letter to her brother, she wrote: 'My Savior is so very precious to me, that I feel I could put my hand in his and go anywhere or do anything ... When I think of how great the harvest and of how few the labourers are I feel like flying. Sometimes I feel as if I had chains on ... If I were a man I believe I would do as Bishop Taylor is doing ... I would travel through the length and breadth of this land and visit every Indian tribe or white settler and miner, and find out their needs, and then hunt up my missionary.' See Susanna Lawrence to her brother, May 30, 1885, ERC.
20 Crosby letter, February 1878, *Missionary Notices* 6, 273.
21 Crosby, *Up and Down the North Pacific Coast*, vii.
22 *Christian Guardian* (September 13, 1893).
23 Green letter, *Christian Guardian* (November 15, 1893).

24 Crosby letter, *Christian Guardian* (November 29, 1893).
25 *Western Methodist Recorder* 13 (1912):6.
26 Crosby's contemporaries could have realized this as well. His letters during his later years revealed frustration on his part. Furthermore, his successors spoke unequivocally about the migratory habits of the people, extreme factionalism, and the recurrence of old habits, especially the potlatch (see Freeman letters, Summer 1903, March 10, 1903 and June 26, 1904; *Missionary Bulletin* 1 (1902-4):221-2, 236, 445-7; and Osterhout letter, December 5, 1902, 89-90). See also Lockner, 'Nineteenth Century British Columbia Methodism,' 137-9, and Greenaway, 'The Challenge of Port Simpson,' 67, 70, 75.
27 Usher's analysis of Duncan (another powerful and domineering individual) also bears evidence of being dominated by the missionary's personality. This problem is intensified by the fact that researchers must make most of their evaluations from missionary literature. There is very scant information available from Native sources and often a large volume of information about the missionary. Hence there is a real danger of seeing things from his viewpoint and of being captivated by his personality. See Usher, *William Duncan of Metlakatla*, Chaps. 3-7.
28 Fisher, 'Henry Williams' Leadership,' 176.
29 Ibid., 196. See also Robin A. Fisher, 'Henry Williams' Leadership of the CMS Mission to New Zealand,' *New Zealand Journal of History* 9 (1975):150.
30 Max A.C. Warren, *Social History and Christian Mission* (London: SCM Press 1967), 195.
31 Crosby, *Up and Down the North Pacific Coast*, 99.
32 Editorial, *Missionary Outlook* 16 (1896):18.
33 H. Alan C. Cairns, *Prelude to Imperialism: British Reactions to Central African Society, 1840-1890* (London: Routledge and Kegan Paul 1965), 78.
34 *Methodist Magazine* 1 (1875):146.
35 Cairns, *Prelude to Imperialism*, 95. Cairns notes that 'all individuals will appear as children if observed and judged from a cultural background irrelevant to their way of life. Similar childish reactions would have been observed in Europeans forced to attune their actions to the intricacies of an African culture, but, as power and technological superiority were in western rather than African hands, adaptation did not proceed in that direction.'
36 Thompson Ferrier, *Our Indians and Their Training For Citizenship* (Toronto: Methodist Mission Rooms, n.d.), 16-18.
37 Ibid., 36. This link between Christianity and civilization is elsewhere documented in such works as Gunson, *Messengers of Grace*, 268-73; Warren, *Social History*, 87-8, 101-8; J.F. Ade Ajayi, *Christian Missions in Nigeria, 1841-1891: The Making of a New Elite* (London: Longmans 1965),

10-18; and Robert F. Berkhofer, Jr., *Salvation and the Savage: An Analysis of Protestant Missions and American Indian Response, 1787-1862* (Lexington: University of Kentucky Press 1965), 4-5, 111-12.
38 Agnes Knight report, Woman's Missionary Society, *Annual Report* (Toronto: Methodist Mission Rooms 1885-6), 57-8.
39 Jennings letter, April 30, 1889, *Missionary Outlook* 9 (1889):128.
40 Ibid.
41 Missionaries have usually been fingered as the worst villains because their emphasis has been on 'directing' social change at their missions.
42 A. Grenfell Price is an excellent example of such a historian. He documents how the coming of the White people doomed Native tribes and their way of life, how Native culture and tribal organization was destroyed by White trade practices, and how Christianity overwhelmed their 'vague' nature worship. While much of this loss was regrettable, such practices as warfare, cannibalism, feuding, torture, abandonment of the sick and aged, and infanticide were eliminated. He then delineates three stages which he claims occur in all contact situations: the first stage is characterized by peaceful opposition, bewilderment, resentment and a sense of loss concerning the old ways; the second involves scorn about the old inferior ways and leads to despondency and depopulation; and the third is characterized by a return to historic beliefs. Implicitly assumed is the notion that this is a universal law regarding White-Native contact, and that Native cultures cannot resist Western ways. See A. Grenfell Price, *White Settlers and Native Peoples: An Historical Study of Racial Contacts between English-speaking Whites and Aboriginal Peoples in the United States, Canada, Australia and New Zealand* (Melbourne, Australia: Georgian House 1949), 196.
43 Usher, *William Duncan of Metlakatla*, 52.
44 Freerk Ch. Kamma, *Koreri, Messianic Movements in the Biak-Numfor Culture Area* (The Hague: Martinus Nijhof 1972), 243.
45 Fisher, 'Henry Williams' Leadership,' 129-33.
46 Gunson, *Messengers of Grace*, 221.
47 K.E. Read, 'Missionary Activities and Social Change in the Central Highlands of Papua and New Guinea,' *South Pacific* 5 (1952):229-38.
48 See page 4, this book.
49 Kamma, *Koreri*, 269.
50 Gunson points out that many missionaries were aware of this: 'Actually the spirituality of the reasons for conversion was not regarded as of supreme importance ... Most had themselves been led to change their lives by similar influences. What mattered in this conversion experience was that the convert became serious in his religious duties, attended all the "means of grace and instruction," adopted the practice of regular prayer, and eventually showed by his changed way of life that

he was ... a regenerate soul.' See Gunson, *Messengers of Grace*, 221.
51 C. Marius Barbeau, *The Downfall of Temlaham*, 6, 12-13, 68, 76-7.
52 George F. Playter, *History of Methodism in Canada* (Toronto: Wesleyan Conference Office 1863), 1:363.
53 Methodist Church of Canada, British Columbia Conference, Port Simpson District, Port Simpson Church Register, 1874-96, UCBCCA.
54 See pages 71-2, this book.
55 Poikail John George, 'Racist Assumptions of the Nineteenth Century Missionary Movement,' *International Review of Missions* 59 (1970):271.
56 J.D.Y. Peel, 'Syncretism and Religious Change,' *Comparative Studies in Society and History* 10 (1967-8):121-41. See also Hilary E. Rumley, 'Reactions to Contact and Colonization: An Interpretation of Religious and Social Change among the Indians in British Columbia' (MA thesis, University of British Columbia 1973), 8-11.
57 John Webster Grant, *Moon of Wintertime* (Toronto: University of Toronto Press 1984), 24.
58 Geertz, *The Interpretation of Cultures*, 6-7.
59 This same phenomenon has been noted by Eugene Genovese in his study of slavery in the United States, where he notes that Christianity gave Black people a sense of cohesion and unity in a paternalistic and intolerable situation. See Eugene D. Genovese, *Roll, Jordan, Roll: The World the Slaves Made* (New York: Random House 1974), 658-60.

Bibliography

PRIMARY SOURCES

Manuscripts and Unpublished Documents and Correspondence

Appleyard, Benjamin. 'Missionary Work among Indians and Fishermen around Post Essington.' Typescript. PABC

Barbeau, C. Marius and William Beynon. Unpublished fieldnotes (selections from the Tsimshian File, compiled by Wilson Duff, in possession of the Museum of Anthropology, University of British Columbia)

Bolton, A.E. Correspondence Inward. Bolton Collection. PABC

–. Diaries, 1884-90. Bolton Collection. PABC

–. Miscellaneous Papers. Bolton Collection. PABC

Bolton, Nellie. Diaries, 1890-1. Bolton Collection. PABC

Canada. Department of Indian Affairs. Black Series. Western Canada, Record Group 10. Microfilm. UBCL

–. Department of Indian Affairs. Deputy Superintendent-General's Letterbooks, 1874-97. Microfilm. UBCL

–. Department of Indian Affairs. Headquarter's Letterbooks, 1874-97. Microfilm. UBCIC

Church Missionary Society. North Pacific Mission. Correspondence, 1857-1900. Microfilm. UBCL

Crosby, Thomas. File. UCBCCA

–. (1894?) Indian Work British Columbia. Handwritten Notes. UCBCCA

Duncan, William. Papers. Microfilm. UBCL

Glad Tidings. Log-book. 1884-90. UCBCCA

Grace United Church, Port Simpson. 'Banquet Speeches Commemorating the Arrival of Rev. Wm. Pollard, the First Ordained Minister to Visit Port Simpson, February 22, 1874.' February 24, 1934. UCBCCA

Bibliography

Hendry, Kate. Letterbook, 1882-9. PABC

Hudson's Bay Company, Fort Simpson, British Columbia. Correspondence Outward, September 1, 1841–October 11, 1844. Signed by John Work. PABC

–. Correspondence Outward, November 20, 1851-November 2, 1855. Signed by Captain W.H. McNeill. PABC

–. Hamilton Moffatt Letterbook, 1859–April 9, 1861 and October 26, 1863–October 24, 1865. PABC

–. Journal, May 12, 1842–June 22, 1843. Kept by John Work and Roderick Finlayson. PABC

–. Journal, September 15, 1859–December 31, 1862. Kept by Hamilton Moffatt and Captain W.H. McNeill. PABC

MacMillan, J.E. Letter to Kate and Alfred Dudoward, October 30, 1873. UCBCCA

Methodist Church of Canada. British Columbia Conference. Fraser River Indian Missions. Indian Methodist Hymnbook. 1898. PABC

–. British Columbia Conference. Port Simpson District. Financial Minutes, 1882-1900. UCBCCA

–. British Columbia Conference. Port Simpson District. Ministerial Sessions, 1881-1900. UCBCCA

–. British Columbia Conference. Port Simpson District. Minutes, 1883-97. UCBCCA

–. British Columbia Conference. Port Simpson District. Port Simpson Church Register, 1874-96. UCBCCA

–. British Columbia Conference. Port Simpson District. Register of Births and Deaths, Marriage Register, 1874-97. UCBCCA

–. British Columbia Conference. Port Simpson District. Stationing Committee Minutes, 1887-1901. UCBCCA

–. Missionary Society. Letterbooks, 1888-98. UCCAT

Morison, Charles. 'Reminiscences of British Columbia from 1862.' Typescript in possession of R. Geddes Large

Raley, G.H. Correspondence Inward. Raley Collection. PABC

–. Miscellaneous, Articles, Papers, etc., Relating to Indians and Missions. Raley Collection. PABC

–. 'Missions and Missionaries of the Methodist Church.' Typescript. Raley Collection. PABC

–. Notes for Speeches and Articles re: Civilization of Indians. Raley Collection. PABC

Robson, Ebenezer, Correspondence Inward. Ebenezer Robson Collection. PABC

–. Diaries, 1897-8. Ebenezer Robson Collection. PABC

–. Extracts from Mission Reports, 1862-94. Ebenezer Robson Collection. PABC

–. Journal of a Voyage on *Glad Tidings*. February 27–March 31, 1889. Ebenezer Robson Collection. PABC
–. Letterbook, 1888-91. Ebenezer Robson Collection. PABC
–. Reminiscences and Miscellaneous Articles. Ebenezer Robson Collection. PABC
Robson, John. Correspondence Inward. John Robson Collection. PABC
Spencer, S.L. Letter Concerning the Beginnings of the Port Simpson Woman's Missionary Society. UCBCCA
Tate, Charles M. File. UCBCCA
Walker (Knight), Agnes. Journal, July 10, 1885–October 23, 1887. PABC
–. 'Narrative of Indian Missionary Recollections.' Typescript. PABC

Published Sources

British Columbia. 1872-1900. *Sessional Papers*. Victoria: R. Wolfenden
–. 1875. *Papers Connected with the Indian Land Question, 1850-1875*. Victoria: R. Wolfenden
–. 1885. *Metlakatla Inquiry, 1884, Report of the Commissioners Together with the Evidence*. Victoria: R. Wolfenden
–. 1885. *Return to an Order . . . for all Correspondence Relating to the Recent Indian Troubles on the North-West Coast*. Victoria: R. Wolfenden
–. 1887. *Report of Conferences between the Provincial Government and Indian Delegates from Fort Simpson and Naas River*. Victoria: R. Wolfenden
–. 1888. *Papers Relating to the Commission Appointed to Enquire into the State and Condition of the Indians of the North-West Coast*. Victoria: R. Wolfenden
Butterworth, Hezekiah. 1890. *Zigzag Journeys in the Great North West*. Boston: Dona Estes
Caamano, Jacinto. 1938. 'The Journal of Jacinto Caamano.' *British Columbia Historical Quarterly* 2:189-222, 126-301
Canada. 1871-1900. Department of Indian Affairs. *Annual Report*. Ottawa: Queen's Printer
Chittenden, Newton H. 1882. *Travels in British Columbia*. Victoria: n.p.
Collison, W.H. 1916. *In the Wake of the War Canoe*. Toronto: Musson
Crosby, Emma. n.d. *How the Gospel Came to Fort Simpson*. Toronto: Woman's Missionary Society of the Methodist Church
Crosby, Thomas. 1906. *David Sallosalton*. Toronto: Department of Missionary Literature of the Methodist Church
–. 1907. *Among the An-ko-me-nums or Flathead Tribes of Indians of the Pacific Coast*. Toronto: William Briggs
–. 1914. *Up and Down the North Pacific Coast by Canoe and Mission Ship*. Toronto: Missionary Society of the Methodist Church
Dunn, John. 1846. *History of the Oregon Territory*. London: Edwards and Hughes

Green, Anson. 1877. *The Life and Times of Rev. Anson Green, Written by Himself, at the Request of the Toronto Conference*. Toronto: Methodist Book Room

Jackson, Sheldon. 1880. *Alaska, and Missions in the North Pacific Coast*. New York: Dodd, Mead

Janvrin, Alice J., ed. 1904. *Snapshots from the North Pacific: Letters Written by the Right Reverend Bishop Ridley*. London: Church Missionary Society

Jennings, Dennis. n.d. *Manners and Customs of the Indians of the Simpson District, British Columbia*. Toronto: Woman's Missionary Society of the Methodist Church

Long, Elizabeth E. and Thomas Crosby. 1907. *How the Light Came to Kitamaat*. Toronto: Woman's Missionary Society of the Methodist Church

Mayne, R.C. 1862. *Four Years in British Columbia and Vancouver Island*. London: J. Murrary

Merk, Frederick. 1931. *Fur Trade and Empire, George Simpson's Journal, Remarks Connected with the Fur Trade in the Course of a Voyage from York Factory to Fort George and Back to York, 1824-1825*. London: Oxford University Press

Methodist Church of Canada. 1874-98. *Journal of Proceedings*. Toronto: n.p.

–. 1874-98. *Minutes of Conferences*. Toronto: n.p.

–. 1875-97. Missionary Society. *Annual Reports*. Toronto: Methodist Mission Rooms

–. 1881-97. Woman's Missionary Society. *Annual Reports*. Toronto: Methodist Mission Rooms

–. 1887-98. British Columbia Conference. *Minutes*. Toronto: n.p.

Methodist Missionary Society. 1889. *Letter from the Methodist Missionary Society to the Superintendent-General of Indian Affairs Respecting British Columbia Troubles*. Toronto: n.p.

[Ogden, Peter Skene?]. 1853. *Traits of American-Indian Life and Character, by a Fur Trader*. London: Smith, Elder

Pierce, W. H. 1933. *From Potlatch to Pulpit*. J.B. Hicks, ed. Vancouver: Vancouver Bindery

Robson, Ebenezer. 1904. *How Methodism Came to British Columbia*. Toronto: Methodist Young People's Forward Movement

St. John, Molyneux. 1877. *The Sea of Mountains, an Account of Lord Dufferin's Tour Through British Columbia in 1876*. 2 vols. London: Hurst and Blackett

Simpson, Sir George. 1847. *Narrative of a Journey Round the World During the Years 1841 and 1842*. 2 vols. London: H. Colburn

Tate, Charles M. n.d. *Our Indian Missions in British Columbia*. Toronto: Methodist Young People's Forward Movement

Taylor, William. 1897. *William Taylor of California, Bishop of Africa: An Autobiography*. London: Hodder and Stoughton

Teichmann, Oskar, ed. 1963. *A Journey to Alaska in the Year 1868: Being a Di-

ary of the Late Emil Teichmann. New York: Argosy-Antiquarian
Tolmie, W.F. 1963. *The Journal of William Fraser Tolmie: Physician and Fur Trader*. Vancouver: Mitchell Press
Wesleyan Methodist Church of Canada. 1861-74. *Minutes of Conferences*. Toronto: Wesleyan Conference Office
Woodsworth, James. 1917. *Thirty Years in the Canadian North-West*. Toronto: McClelland, Goodchild and Stewart
Work, John. 1945. *The Journal of John Work, January to October, 1835*. Archives of British Columbia, Memoir No. 10. Victoria: King's Printer

Newspapers and Contemporary Periodicals

British Columbian. 1883. New Westminster
Canadian Methodist Magazine (also *Methodist Magazine and Review*). 1875-98. Toronto
Christian Guardian. 1873-97. Toronto
Daily Colonist (also *British Colonist* or *British Daily Colonist*). 1863-97, 1975. Victoria
Home and School. 1884-94. Toronto
Missionary Bulletin. 1902-4. Toronto
Missionary Notices of the Methodist Church of Canada. January, 1875–August, 1878. Toronto
Missionary Outlook. 1881-97. Toronto
Onward. 1893-6. Toronto
The Province. 1909, 1929, and 1958. Vancouver
Wesleyan Methodist Notices. 1869-72. Toronto
(Western) Methodist Recorder. 1899-1920. Victoria

SECONDARY SOURCES

Published Books

Adams, John W. 1973. *The Gitksan Potlatch*. Toronto, Montreal: Holt, Rinehart and Winston
Ajayi, J.F. Ade. 1965. *Christian Missions in Nigeria, 1841-1891: The Making of a New Elite*. London: Longmans
Arctander, J.W. 1909.*The Apostle of Alaska*. New York: Fleming H. Revell
Armstrong, Anthony. 1973. *The Church of England, the Methodists and Society, 1700-1850*. London: University of London Press
Bangs, Nathan. 1838-41. *History of the Methodist Episcopal Church*. 4 vols. New York: Mason and Lane
Barbeau, C. Marius. 1961. *Tsimsyan Myths*. National Museum of Canada,

Bulletin No. 174. Ottawa: Queen's Printer
—. 1973. *The Downfall of Temlaham*. Edmonton: Hurtig
Barnett, H.G. 1953. *Innovation: The Basis of Cultural Change*. New York: McGraw-Hill
Begg, Alexander. 1901. *A Sketch of the Successful Missionary Work of William Duncan, 1858-1901*. Victoria: n.p.
Berkhofer, Robert F., Jr. 1965. *Salvation and the Savage: An Analysis of Protestant Missions and American Indian Response, 1787-1862*. Lexington: University of Kentucky Press
Binney, Judith. 1968. *The Legacy of Guilt: A Life of Thomas Kendall*. London and Auckland: Auckland-Oxford University Press
Boas, Franz. 1909-10. *Tsimshian Mythology*. Washington, DC: Bureau of American Enthnology, 31st Annual Report, 29-1037
Cail, Robert E. 1974. *Land, Man, and the Law: The Disposal of Crown Lands in British Columbia, 1871-1913*. Vancouver: University of British Columbia Press
Cairns, H. Alan C. 1965. *Prelude to Imperialism: British Reactions to Central African Society, 1840-1890*. London: Routledge and Kegan Paul
Caldwell, John W. 1967. *The Unification of Methodism in Canada, 1865-1884*. Bulletin 19, Committee on Archives. Toronto: United Church Publishing House
Carroll, John. 1874. *Case and His Contemporaries*. 5 vols. Toronto: Wesleyan Conference Office
[Church Missionary Society]. 1899. *Metlakatla: Ten Years' Work among the Tsimsheean Indians*. London: Church Missionary Society
—. 1899. *One Hundred Years: Being the Short History of the Church Missionary Society*. London: Church Missionary Society
Clark, S.D. 1948. *Church and Sect in Canada*. Toronto: University of Toronto Press
Cornish, George Henry. 1903. *Cyclopedia of Methodism in Canada*. 2 vols. Toronto: Methodist Book and Publishing House
Cragg, G.R., G. French, and J.W. Grant. 1968. *Christianity and the Development of Canadian Culture*. Hamilton: McMaster Divinity College
Craig, Gerald M. 1963. *Upper Canada, the Formative Years*. Toronto: McClelland and Stewart
Davis, E.A., ed. 1925. *Commemorative Review of Methodist, Presbyterian and Congregational Churches in British Columbia*. Vancouver: Joseph Lee
Davis, George. 1904. *Metlakatla: A True Narrative of the Red Man*. Chicago: Ram's Horn Company
Drucker, Philip. 1955. *Indians of the North West Coast*. Garden City: Natural History Press
—. 1965. *Cultures of the North Pacific Coast*. San Francisco: Chandler
Duff, Wilson. 1965. *The Indian History of British Columbia: Vol. I, The Impact of*

the White Man. Anthropology in British Columbia Memoir No. 5. Victoria: Provincial Museum

Edwards, Maldwyn Lloyd. 1933. *John Wesley and the Eighteenth Century, A Study of His Social and Political Influence*. London: George Allen and Unwin

Elgee, William H. 1964. *The Social Teachings of the Canadian Churches*. Toronto: Ryerson Press

Eliade, Mircea. 1963. *Myth and Reality, World Perspectives*. W.R. Trask, trans. New York: Harper and Row

Ferrier, Thompson. n.d. *Our Indians and their Training for Citizenship*. Toronto: Methodist Mission Rooms

Fisher, Robin. 1977. *Contact and Conflict: Indian-European Relations in British Columbia, 1774-1890*. Vancouver: University of British Columbia Press

Frankfort, Henri, Mrs. H.A. Frankfort, John A. Wilson, and Thorkild Jacobsen, eds. 1971. *Before Philosophy*. Baltimore: Penguin

French, Goldwin. 1962. *Parsons and Politics: The Role of the Wesleyan Methodists in Upper Canada and the Maritimes from 1780-1855*. Toronto: Ryerson Press

Garfield, Viola E. 1931. *Changes in the Marriage Customs of the Tsimshian*. Seattle: University of Washington Press

–. 1939. *Tsimshian Clan and Society*. Seattle: University of Washington Press

– and Paul S. Wingert. 1966. *The Tsimshian Indians and Their Arts*. Seattle: University of Washington Press

Geertz, Clifford. 1973. *The Interpretation of Cultures*. New York: Basic Books

Genovese, Eugene D. 1974. *Roll, Jordon, Roll: The World the Slaves Made*. New York: Random House

Goldman, Irving. 1975. *The Mouth of Heaven: An Introduction to Kwakiutl Religious Thought*. New York: John Wiley

Grant, John Webster. 1972. *The Church in the Canadian Era*. Toronto, Montreal: McGraw-Hill Ryerson

–, ed. 1963. *The Churches and the Canadian Experience: A Faith and Order Study of the Christian Tradition*. Toronto: Ryerson Press

–. *Moon of Wintertime*. 1984. Toronto: University of Toronto Press

Gunson, Niel. n.d. *Australian Reminiscences and Papers of L.E. Threlkeld*. Australian Aboriginal Studies No. 40, Ethnohistory Series No. 2. Canberra: Australian Institute of Aboriginal Studies

–. 1978. *Messengers of Grace: Evangelical Missionaries in the South Seas, 1797-1860*. New York: Oxford University Press

Halevy, Elie. 1971. *The Birth of Methodism in England*. B. Semmel, trans. Chicago: University of Chicago Press

Hawthorne, H.B., C.S. Belshaw, and S.M. Jamieson. 1958. *The Indians of British Columbia: A Study of Contemporary Social Adjustment*. Toronto: University of Toronto Press

Herskovits, Melville J. 1938. *Acculturation: The Study of Culture Contact*. New York: J.J. Augustin

Johnson, Charles A. 1955. *The Frontier Camp Meeting*. Dallas: Southern Methodist University Press

Kamma, Freerk Ch. 1972. *Koreri, Messianic Movements in the Biak-Numfor Culture Area*. The Hague: Martinus Nijhoff

Knight, Rolf. 1978. *Indians at Work: An Informal History of Native Indian Labour in British Columbia, 1858-1930*. Vancouver: New Star Books

Knorr, Klaus E. 1964. *British Colonial Theories, 1570-1850*. Toronto: University of Toronto Press

Knox, Ronald A. 1952. *Enthusiasm: A Chapter in the History of Religion with Special Reference to the XVII and XVIII Centuries*. Oxford: Clarendon Press

Landon, Fred. 1967. *Western Ontario and the American Frontier*. Toronto: McClelland and Stewart

Large, R. Geddes. 1957. *The Skeena, River of Destiny*. Vancouver: Mitchell Press

LaViolette, Forrest. 1961. *The Struggle for Survival: Indian Cultures and the Protestant Ethic in British Columbia*. Toronto: University of Toronto Press

Lee, Umphrey. 1967. *The Historical Backgrounds of Early Methodist Enthusiasm*. New York: AMS

Linton, Ralph, ed. 1963. *Acculturation in Seven American Indian Tribes*. Gloucester, MA: Peter Smith

MacLean, John. 1919. *Vanguards of Canada*. Toronto: Methodist Publishing House

Magney, William H. 1968. *The Methodist Church and the National Gospel*. Bulletin 20, Committee on Archives. Toronto: United Church Publishing House

Malinowski, Bronislaw. 1945. *The Dynamics of Culture Change: An Inquiry into Race Relations in Africa*. P. Kaberry, ed. London: Oxford University Press

–. 1954. *Magic, Science and Religion, and other Essays*. Garden City: Doubleday

Martin, Calvin. 1978. *Keepers of the Game*. Berkeley and Los Angeles: University of California Press

[Methodist Church of Canada]. 1891. *Centennial of Canadian Methodism*. Toronto: William Briggs

–. 1924. *Faith of our Fathers, the Story of One Hundred Years of Victory*. Toronto: n.p.

Moeran, J.W.W. 1923. *McCullagh of Aiyansh*. London: Marshall Bros.

Miller, Joy and Carol M. Eastman, eds. 1984. *The Tsimshian and Their Neighbours of the North Pacific Coast*. Seattle: University of Washington Press

Moir, John S. 1972. *The Church in the British Era*. Toronto, Montreal: McGraw-Hill Ryerson

Bibliography

–, ed. 1966. *The Cross in Canada*. Toronto: Ryerson Press

Morley, Alan. 1967. *Roar of the Breakers, A Biography of Peter Kelly*. Toronto: Ryerson

Morris, Wilfred H. 1941. *Captain Oliver, a Fisher of Man*. Trujillo, Peru: Casa Evangelica de Publicaciones

Morton, W.L., ed. 1968. *The Shield of Achilles: Aspects of Canada in the Victorian Age*. Toronto: McClelland and Stewart

Moyer, Kenneth A. 1974. *My Saddle was My Study: The Story of the Methodist Saddlebag Preachers of Upper Canada*. Elmira, ON: n.p.

Neill, Stephen. 1964. *A History of Christian Missions*. Hammondsworth: Penguin

–. 1966. *Colonialism and Christian Missions*. New York: McGraw-Hill

Niblack, A.P. 1890. *The Coast Indians of Southern Alaska and Northern British Columbia*. United States National Museum Annual Report, 1888. Washington, DC: n.p.

Niebuhr, H. Richard. 1929. *The Social Sources of Denominationalism*. New York: World Publishing

Owens, J.M.R. 1974. *Prophets in the Wilderness: The Wesleyan Mission to New Zealand, 1819-1827*. Auckland: Auckland University Press

Patterson, E. Palmer, II. 1972. *The Canadian Indian: A History since 1500*. Don Mills: Collier-Macmillan

Peake, Frank A. 1959. *The Anglican Church in British Columbia*. Vancouver: Mitchell Press

Platt, H. L. and E.S. Strachan. 1908-17. *The Story of the Years: A History of the Woman's Missionary Society of the Methodist Church of Canada, 1886-1916*. 3 vols. Toronto: Woman's Missionary Society

Playter, George F. 1862. *History of Methodism in Canada*. Vol. 1. Toronto: Wesleyan Conference Office

Polanyi, Michael. 1975. *Meaning*. Chicago and London: University of Chicago Press

Price, A. Grenfell. 1949. *White Settlers and Native Peoples: An Historical Study of Racial Contacts between English-speaking Whites and Aboriginal Peoples in the United States, Canada, Australia and New Zealand*. Melbourne: Georgian House

Pringle, G.O.F. n.d. *In Great Waters*. Toronto: Ryerson Press

Raunet, Daniel. 1984. *Without Surrender, Without Consent: A History of Nishga Land Claims*. Vancouver: Douglas and McIntyre

Rich, E.E. 1959. *The History of the Hudson's Bay Company, 1670-1870*. Vol. 2, 1763-1870. London: Hudson's Bay Record Society

Robinson, Will. 1962. *Men of Medeek*. Kitimat: Northern Sentinel Press

Rosman, Abraham and Paula G. Rubel. 1971. *Feasting With Mine Enemy: Rank and Exchange among North West Coast Societies*. New York and London: Columbia University Press

Rowe, Kenneth E., ed. 1976. *The Place of Wesley in the Christian Tradition.* Metuchen, NJ: Scarecrow Press

Runnalls, F.E. 1974. *It's God's Country: A Review of the United Church and its Founding Partners in the Congregational, Methodist and Presbyterian Churches in British Columbia.* Vancouver: United Church of Canada, British Columbia Conference, Committee on Archives

Ryerson, A. Egerton. 1882. *Canadian Methodism: Its Epochs and Characteristics.* Toronto: William Briggs

Sanderson, Joseph E. 1916. *The First Century of Methodism in Canada.* 2 vols. Toronto: William Briggs

Saum, Lewis O. 1963. *The Fur Trade and the Indian.* Seattle and London: University of Washington Press

Scholefield, E.O.S. and F.W. Howay. 1914. *British Columbia from the Earliest Times to the Present.* 4 vols. Vancouver: S.J. Clarke

Scott, Robert C. 1947. *My Captain Oliver: A Story of Two Missionaries on the British Columbia Coast.* Toronto: United Church of Canada

Seguin, Margaret, ed. 1984. *The Tsimshian: Images of the Past, Views for the Present.* Vancouver: University of British Columbia Press

Semmel, Bernard. 1973. *The Methodist Revolution.* New York: Basic Books

Smith, Timothy Laurence. 1957. *Revivalism and Social Reform.* New York: Abington Press

Stephenson, Mrs. F.E. n.d. *One Hundred Years of Canadian Methodist Missionaries.* Toronto: Missionary Society of the Methodist Church

Stock, Eugene. 1881. *Metlakahtla and the North Pacific Mission of the Church Missionary Society.* London: Church Missionary Society

–. 1899. *The History of the Church Missionary Society, its Environment, its Men and its Work.* Vols. 2 and 3. London: Church Missionary Society

Sutherland, Alexander. 1904. *Methodism in Canada.* Toronto: Methodist Mission Rooms

–. n.d. *The Methodist Church and Missions in Canada.* n.d. Toronto: Department of Missionary Literature of the Methodist Church

Sweet, William W. 1946. *Religion on the American Frontier, 1783-1840.* Vol. 4, 'The Methodists.' Chicago: n.p.

Taylor, Ernest Richard. 1935. *Methodism and Politics, 1791-1851.* Cambridge: Cambridge University Press

Usher, Jean. 1974. *William Duncan of Metlakatla: A Victorian Missionary in British Columbia.* National Museum of Man Publication in History, No. 5. Ottawa: National Museum of Canada

Wa, Gisday and Delgam Uukw n.d. *The Spirit in the Land.* Gabriola: Reflections

Walsh, Henry Horace. 1956. *The Christian Church in Canada.* Toronto: Ryerson Press

Walsh, J.D. and G.V. Bennett, eds. 1966. *Essays in Modern Church History: In*

Memory of Norman Sykes. London: Black
Warner, Wellman J. 1930. *The Wesleyan Movement in the Industrial Revolution*. London: Longmans
Warren, Max A.C. 1954. *Revival: An Enquiry*. London: SCM Press
–. 1965. *The Missionary Movement from Britain in Modern History*. London: SCM Press
–. 1967. *Social History and Christian Mission*. London: SCM Press
Wellcome, H.S. 1887. *The Story of Metlakahtla*. New York: Saxon and Co.
Withrow, William H., ed. 1895. *The Native Races of North America*. Toronto: Methodist Mission House
Worsley, Peter. 1968. *The Trumpet Shall Sound: A Study of 'Cargo Cults' in Melanesia*. New York: Schockem Books
Wright, Harrison M. 1959. *New Zealand, 1769-1840, Early Years of Western Contact*. Cambridge, MA: Harvard University Press
Zaslow, Morris. 1971. *The Opening of the Canadian North*. Toronto: McClelland and Stewart

Published Periodical Articles

Barbeau, C. Marius. 1915. 'Growth and Federation in the Tsimshian Phratries.' International Congress of Americanists, *Proceedings* 19:402-8
–. 1917. 'Review of Boas' Tsimshian Mythology.' *American Anthropologist* 19:548-63
–. 1930. 'Totem Poles: A Recent Art of the North West Coast of America.' *Geographic Review* 20:258-72
–. 1940. 'Old Port Simpson.' *The Beaver* 271:20-3
Barnett, H.G. 1941. 'Personal Conflicts and Cultural Change.' *Social Forces* 20:160-71
–. 1942. 'Invention and Cultural Change.' *American Anthropologist* 44:14-30
–. 1942. 'Applied Anthropology in 1860.' *Applied Anthropology* 1:19-32
Berkhofer, Robert F., Jr. 1963. 'Protestants, Pagans and Sequence among the North American Indians, 1760-1860.' *Ethnohistory* 10:201-22
Beynon, William. 1941. 'The Tsimshian of Metlakatla, Alaska.' *American Anthropologist* 43:83-8
Binney, Judith. 1969. 'Christianity and the Maoris to 1840: A Comment.' *New Zealand Journal of History* 3:143-65
Blackman, Margaret. 1977. 'Continuity and Change in Northwest Coast Ceremonialism: Introduction.' *Arctic Anthropology* 14:1-5
Boas, Franz. 1924. 'The Social Organization of the Tribes of the North Pacific Coast.' *American Anthropologist* 26:323-32
Brown, G. Gordon. 1944. 'Missions and Social Diffusion.' *American Journal of Sociology* 50:214-19
Dorsey, G.A. 1897. 'The Geography of the Tsimshian Indians.' Monograph

reprinted from *The American Antiquarian*

Dougall, J.W.C. 1946. 'The Reason for Medical Missions.' *International Review of Missions* 35:251-5

Drucker, Philip. 1939. 'Rank, Wealth and Kinship in North West Coast Society.' *American Anthropologist* 41:55-65

Duff, Wilson. 1964. 'Contributions of Marius Barbeau to West Coast Ethnology.' *Anthropologica* 6:63-96

English, John C. 1969. 'John Wesley and the Anglican Moderates of the Seventeenth Century.' *Anglican Theological Review* 51:203-20

Fisher, Robin A. 1975. 'Henry Williams' Leadership of the Church Missionary Society Mission to New Zealand.' *New Zealand Journal of History* 9:142-153

Furst, Peter T. 1973-4. 'Roots and Continuities.' *Arts Canada* 184-7:33-60

George, Poikail John. 1970. 'Racist Assumptions of the Nineteenth Century Missionary Movement.' *International Review of Missions* 59:271-84

Gewehr, Wesley M. 1928. 'Some Factors in the Expansion of Frontier Methodism, 1800-1811.' *Journal of Religion* 8:98-120

Grumet, Robert S. 1975. 'Changes in the Coast Tsimshian Redistributive Activities in the Fort Simpson Region of British Columbia, 1788-1862.' *Ethnohistory* 22:295-318

Gunther, Erna. 1926. 'An Analysis of the First Salmon Ceremony.' *American Anthropologist* 28:605-17

–. n.d. 'A Further Analysis of the First Salmon Ceremony.' *University of Washington Publications in Anthropology* 2:129-73

Howay, F.W. 1942. 'The Introduction of Intoxicating Liquors amongst the Indians of the North West Coast.' *British Columbia Historical Quarterly* 6:157-69

LaViolette, Forrest E. 1951. 'Missionaries and the Potlatch.' *Queen's Quarterly* 58:237-51

Martin, Calvin. 1978. 'Ethno-history: A Better Way to Write Indian History.' *Western Historical Quarterly* 9:41-56

Owens, J.M.R. 1968. 'Christianity and the Maoris till 1840.' *New Zealand Journal of History* 2:18-40

Peel, J.D.Y. 1967-8. 'Syncretism and Religious Change.' *Comparative Studies in Society and History* 10:121-41

Read, K.E. 1952. 'Missionary Activities and Social Change in the Central Highlands of Papua and New Guinea.' *South Pacific* 5:229-38

Rettig, Andrew. 1980. 'A Nativist Movement at Metlakatla Mission.' *BC Studies* 46:28-39

Sheehan, Bernard W. 1969. 'Indian-White Relations in Early America: A Review Essay.' *William and Mary Quarterly* 26:267-86

Stanley, George F.G. 1952. 'The Indian Background of Canadian History.' *Canadian Historical Association, Report* 14-21

Usher, Jean. 1971. 'Apostles and Aborigines: The Social Theory of the Church Missionary Society.' *Social History* 7:28-52

Walker, James St. G. 1971. 'The Indian in Canadian Historical Writing.' Canadian Historical Association, *Historical Papers* 21-51

Zaslow, Morris. 1966. 'The Missionary as Social Reformer: The Case of William Duncan.' *Journal of the Canadian Church Historical Society* 8:52-69

Unpublished Material

Brooks, William H. 1972. 'Methodism in the Canadian West in the Nineteenth Century.' PHD dissertation, University of Manitoba

Burnyeat, John P. 1973. 'Methodist Marine Missions in British Columbia, 1884-1924.' Master of Christian Studies thesis, Regent College

Darling, John D. 1955. 'The Effects of Culture Contact on the Tsimshian System of Land Tenure During the Nineteenth Century.' MA thesis, University of British Columbia

Finlay, J. Malcolm. 1956. 'The Nature of Methodism in Upper Canada in the Mid-Nineteenth Century, with Particular Reference to the Christian Guardian.' MA thesis, Queen's University

Fisher, Robin A. 1969. 'Henry Williams' Leadership of the Church Missionary Society Mission in New Zealand, 1823-1840.' MA thesis, University of Auckland

Greenaway, Archibald M. 1955. 'The Challenge of Port Simpson.' BD essay, Union College

Hacker, George C. 1933. 'The Methodist Church in British Columbia, 1859-1900.' BA essay, University of British Columbia

Halpin, Marjorie M. 1973. 'The Tsimshian Crest System: A Study Based on Museum Specimens and the Marius Barbeau and William Beynon Field Notes.' PHD dissertation, University of British Columbia

Lane, Barbara S. 1953. 'A Comparative and Analytical Study of Some Aspects of North West Coast Religion.' PHD thesis, University of Washington

Lindstrom, Erling G. 1972. 'The Methodist Church, Canada, 1884-1912.' MA thesis, Simon Fraser University

Lockner, Bradley J. 1975. 'Nineteenth Century British Columbia Methodism: The Missionary Enterprise of Thomas Crosby.' Master of Christian Studies thesis, Regent College

Pritchard, John. 1977. 'Economic Development and the Disintegration of the Traditional Culture Among the Haisla.' PHD dissertation, University of British Columbia

Reid, Katerina S. 1976. 'The Origins of the Tsetseqa in the Baxus: A Study of Kwakiutl Prayers, Myths and Ritual.' PHD dissertation, University of British Columbia

Robinson, Michael. 1973. 'Great Men in the North West Coast Small Societies: Legaik, Cuneah and Maquinna.' BA essay, University of British Columbia

Rumley, Hilary E. 1973. 'Reactions to Contact and Colonization: An Interpretation of Religious and Social Change among the Indians of British Columbia.' MA thesis, University of British Columbia

Young, Walter D. 1955. 'Pioneer Methodist Missionaries in British Columbia, 1859-1871.' BA essay, University of British Columbia

Index

Alcohol, viii, 16-17, 21, 24, 63
Anglican Church, 20, 28-30, 39, 42-3, 54, 83, 86, 102
Anthropology, Tsimshian people. *See* Tsimshian: culture
Arminianism, 29
Augustine, 28
Awakening (1858), 27, 33
Aztec nation, vii

Band of Christian Workers. *See* Tsimshian: Band of Christian Workers
Baptism: by Crosby and Methodists, 41, 46; by Duncan, 22
Barbeau, Marius, 4, 107, 117-18 n.2
Barnett, H.G., 96
Bennett, Sam, 53
Beynon, William, 53
Binney, Judith, 95
Boarding homes/schools, 103. *See also* Boys' Institute; Crosby Girls' Home
Boas, Franz, 4, 117-18 n.2
Bolton, Dr. A.E., 64, 90
Boys' Institute, 64
Brass Band, 50, 70
British Columbia, government of, 43, 64, 66, 111; Joint Commission of 1887, 80-3; and land question, 72-87; view of Northwest Coast missionaries, 77-8, 81-6
British Wesleyan Methodist Church. *See* Methodist Church, British Wesleyan
Bryant, Cornelius, 34

Calvin, John, 28
Camaano, Jacinto, 15
Canada, government of, 64, 66, 111; Department of Indian Affairs, 75, 83-5; Indian Advancement Act, 78, 80-3, 87, 89-90; Joint Commission of 1887, 80-3; and land question in Northwest Coast, 72-87; view of Northwest Coast missionaries, 77-8, 81-6
Canadian Pacific Railway, 74-5, 92
Cannibal society, 12, 40. *See also* Tsimshian: winter ceremonies
Catholic Society, Roman, viii, 102
Champlain, Samuel de, viii
Chilliwack, 35-6, 40, 44
Chippewa, 108
Christian Guardian, 28, 33, 57, 99
'Christian Street,' 35
Christianizing aim of missions. *See* Missionaries

Christmas celebration, 70
Church Army, 55
Church Missionary Society (Anglican), 3, 20, 40-2, 53-5, 78, 82, 101
Civilizing aim of missions. *See* Missionaries
Coast Tsimshian, 15, 16, 25. *See also* Tsimshian
Collison, William, 40-1, 54
Conversion, 105-9, 111; definition, 106. *See also* Culture
Cornwall, Clement J., 80, 82, 86
Crosby (nee Douse), Emma, 36, 63, 98-9
Crosby, Thomas, 3, 39, 41, 90, 94, 107; appointment to Fort Simpson, 36; arrival at Fort Simpson, 42; background, 25-8; and Band of Christian Workers, power struggle with, 50-4 (*see also* Tsimshian: Band of Christian Workers); and class meetings, 36, 45, 47 (*see also* Methodism: class meetings); and conflict with Duncan, 42-4; decline of support for in 1890s, 92-4; and education, 41, 61-3, 71, 108; evaluation of mission, 109; first years in British Columbia, 34-6; and frustration with course of mission, 45-50, 67-71, 92-4, 127 n.47; and itinerant system, mobility, 37, 45, 48-9, 71, 131 n.37; land question role, 73-5, 77-8, 80-4, 87 (*see also* British Columbia, government of; Canada, government of; Methodist Church of Canada: and land question; Tsimshian: and land question); and medicine, 64-5; and Methodist Missionary Society conflict, 56-9 (*see also* Methodist Missionary Society); mission vocation, x-xi, 28, 36-7, 56-7; personality role, 97-101; revivalistic focus, 35-7, 44-8, 54 (*see also* Revivalism; Tsimshian: response to Crosby's revivalism); and rift with Bishop Ridley, 54-5; and secular life, program for, 61-67; view of Native cultures, 34-5, 65-9, 102, 110; and village council, 89 (*see also* Tsimshian: village council)
Crosby Girls' Home, 63-4, 103
Culture: defined, 4-5, 119 n.31; and relationship to conversion, 106; and relationship to religion and myths, 10; and relationship to social system, 4-5, 10; and relationship (of culture, religion, social system) to Tsimshian, 14, 20, 25, 37-8, 59-60, 93, 106-7
Cuyler, R.B., 50

Dancing Societies, 12. *See also* Tsimshian: winter ceremonies
Davie, Alexander, 78
Deans, James, 85
Destroyer society, 12. *See also* Tsimshian: winter ceremonies
Dewdney, Edgar (Superintendent-General of Indian Affairs 1889), 85-6
Dog-eater society, 12. *See also* Tsimshian: winter ceremonies
Douglas, James, 85-6
Douse, Emma J. *See* Crosby, Emma
Downfall of Temlaham (Marius Barbeau), 107
Drucker, Philip, 7-8, 18, 119-20 n.41
Dudoward, Alfred, 39-40, 48, 51, 54, 76-7, 82-3, 88
Dudoward, Kate, 39-40, 42, 54, 62
Duff, Wilson, 7
Dufferin, Lord, Governor-General

of Canada, 73, 75, 77, 83, 85-6
Duncan, William, 3, 16, 26, 39, 54, 62, 77-8, 81, 84-5, 96, 104-5; background, 20-1; and conflict with Methodism and Crosby, 40-4; and education of Natives, 21-3; and Indian Reserve policy, 72; and medicine, 23; mission philosophy, 21-5

Edgecome, Ensign, 53
Education. *See* Crosby, Thomas; Duncan, William; Missionaries; Tsimshian
Eliade, Mircea, 10
Elliot, A.C. (Stipendary Magistrate), 77, 81, 87
Epworth League, 53
Essington, Port, 53-4, 64

Family, nuclear. *See* Crosby: and secular life; Duncan: mission philosophy
Firefighting Corps, 50
Firethrower society, 12. *See also* Tsimshian: winter ceremonies
Fisher, Robin, ix, xii, 18, 23, 101, 108
Fort Nass. *See* Nass, Fort
Fort Simpson. *See* Simpson, Fort
Fort Simpson Post Journal, 18, 21, 23
Frankfort, Henri, ix
Fur trade, viii. *See also* Hudson's Bay Company; Tsimshian: trade with Europeans

Garfield, Viola E., 69
Gazette, 75-6
Geertz, Clifford, 4-5, 10, 93, 106-7, 110
Georgetown, 66
Gitands Tribe, 39
Gitksan, 5, 15-16, 78
Gitksan, Wet'suweten land claim, 9

Glad Tidings (ship), 49-50, 53-6
Gold rush of 1858, 22
Goldman, Irving, 8-9
Good, Rev. J.B., 42
Gosnell, Louis, 76
Governments. *See* British Columbia, government of; Canada, government of
Grant, John Webster, 110
Green, A.E., 47, 50-1, 55, 73, 83, 88, 99
Greenaway, Archibald, 48, 55, 100
Grey, Lewis, 69
Gunson, Neil, 28, 98, 108

Hahis, Chief, 42
Haida, 15-16, 21
Hall, Rev. A.J., 43
Hall, Robert Hanley, MP, 87
Halpin, Marjorie, 12
Hart, Matron, 63
'Heathen Street,' 35
Hendry, Kate, 63-4
Historiography on Native/European relations, ix-xi, 95-109, 140 n.42. *See also* Tsimshian: analysis of response to missions
Home and School, 58
Horne, Melville, 34
Hudson's Bay Company, viii, 21, 24, 41, 74-5, 81, 85-6; trade with Tsimshian, 16-20
Huron Nation, viii

Indian Advancement Act. *See* Canada, government of: Department of Indian Affairs; Tsimshian: and Indian Advancement Act
Indian Reserve Policy. *See* British Columbia, government of; Canada, government of: Department of Indian Affairs

Jennings, Dennis, 50-1, 83, 104
Jesuits, viii
Johnston, Matthew, 42, 92
Jones, Peter, 53
Journal of Education, 33

Kamma, Freerk Ch., 105-6
Kennedy, Dr. John, 15-16
Kincolith, 43, 82
Knight, Agnes, 98-9, 104
Knight, Rolf, 92
Kwakiutl, 8-9, 13

Land question. *See* British Columbia, government of: and land question; Canada, government of: and land question; Crosby: and land question; Methodist Church of Canada: and land question; Tsimshian: and land question
Large, R. Geddes, 53
Leask, David, 81
Legaic (Chief), 15-16, 39, 85
Legaic, Paul, 77
Lockner, Bradley, 48, 55, 100

McCullagh, Rev. J.B., 54
Macdonald, Prime Minister John A. (Superintendent-General of Indian Affairs), 75, 80, 82, 84-5
MacKay, J.W. (Indian Agent), 76-7
McNeill, William, 17
Maori, 101
Maple Bay, 36
Martin, Calvin, ix, 19-20
Medicine. *See* Crosby; Duncan
Methodism, x, 6, 25, 102; appeal to Tsimshian, 39-41; beginnings in Britain, 28-30; in Canada, 31-4, 57-8; class meetings, 29, 31 (*see also* Crosby: and class meetings); program at Fort Simpson, 45; and revivalism (*see* Crosby: and revivalism; Revivalism); in United States, 30-1
Methodist Church, British Wesleyan, 31-2
Methodist Church of Canada (Wesleyan Methodist Church before Union of 1883-4), 53, 56; and conflict with Band of Christian Workers, 52-4 (*see also* Band of Christian Workers); and land question, 84-6
Methodist Church of Canada, British Columbia Conference, 84, 94; membership records at Port Simpson, 108; Ministerial Sessions, 52-3, 84; Port Simpson Register, 48, appendix
Methodist Church, Wesleyan (became Methodist Church of Canada after union of 1883-4), 25, 27-8, 31-2, 41-2, 44, 54
Methodist Episcopal Church (United States), 31
Methodist Missionary Society, 51, 58, 64, 85-6, 99. *See also* Crosby: and Methodist Missionary Society conflict
Methodist Recorder, 97
Metlakatla, 73; and conflict with Methodists, 39-44; co-operation with governments, 82-4, 86; and land question, 76, 78; as model village, 22-5, 62, 72, 96-7, 105
Metlakatla, New, 44
Metlakatla Inquiry of 1884, 77-8
Metlakatla Pass, 6
Mills, David (Superintendent-General of Indian Affairs), 67
Missionaries: aims generally in North America, viii-xi; Christianizing aim, vii-viii, x, 21, 26, 34-5, 61; civilizing aim,

vii-viii, x, 21, 26, 34-5, 61; and education, role of, 103; interpretations of role of, 95-102, 106-7, 109; views generally of Native cultures, viii-ix, 102-4
Missionary Outlook, 57, 102
Moffatt, Hamilton, 21

Nanaimo, 34-5, 50
Nass, Fort, 15
Nass, region of, 6, 45, 73-5, 80-1, 89, 92
Nelson, Chief Albert, 49, 71
New Metlakatla. *See* Metlakatla, New
New Year's celebration, 44, 50, 70
New Zealand, 95, 97, 101
Niebuhr, H. Richard, 32
Nishga, 5, 15-16, 78

Oliver, Captain William, 53
O'Reilly, Peter (Indian Reserve Commissioner), 74-7, 79, 84, 86, 90
Osterhout, Rev. S.S., 55
Ottawa, 84, 89
Owens, J.M.R., 97

Peel, J.D.Y., 110
Pelagianism, 29
Pickering, Yorkshire, 26
Piercy, George, 27-8
Planta, J.B. (Commissioner), 80
Playter, George, 108
Pollard, Rev. William, 41-2, 45, 62, 73
Port Essington. *See* Essington, Port
Port Simpson. *See* Simpson, Port
Port Simpson Industrial Fair, 66
Powell, I.W. (Indian Superintendent), 65, 74-8, 83, 86-7
Private property, 68-70. *See* Crosby: and secular life; Duncan: mission philosophy
Prostitution, 17, 21, 63

Raley, George E., 56, 90
Ralph, Mr., 76
Read, K.E., 106
Recollets, viii
Reid, Katerina S., 13, 19
Religion. *See* Crosby: mission vocation, revivalistic focus, view of Native cultures; Culture; Duncan: mission philosophy; Revivalism; Tsimshian: religion
Revivalism, 6, 26-34, 39-40, 43, 46. *See also* Crosby: revivalistic focus; Revivals at Port Simpson
Revivals at Port Simpson, in 1874, 44-5; in 1877, 43, 46; in 1881-2, 46; in 1892-3, 47-8
Richards, Charles M., 63
Ridley, Bishop William, 44, 53-5, 77-8, 81, 84
Rifle Corps, 50, 70
Robson, Rev. Ebenezer, 46, 54, 56, 83, 94
Robson, John (Commissioner of Lands and Works), 78
Roman Catholic Church. *See* Catholic Church, Roman
Ryerson, Egerton, 31, 33

Sallosalton, David, 36
Salvation Army, 47-8, 53-6, 90-1, 93, 111
Seguin, Margaret, 13
Semmel, Bernard, 33
Sepulveda, de, vii-viii
Shakes, Chief, 88
Shepherd, Matthew, 72
Sifton, Clifford, 90
Simpson, Fort (changed to Port Simpson, 1880), xi, 3, 16-7, 21-6, 36-7; arrival of Duncan in, 20; and

Crosby mission, 'religious' life, 39-44; move from, to Metlakatla, 22-3
Simpson, Port (changed from Fort Simpson, 1880), 98-100, 104, 107-9, 111; and Crosby mission, 'religious' life, 44-60; and Crosby mission, 'secular' life, 61-94
Simpson, Sir George, 15
Skeena region, 5, 45, 48, 54, 74-5, 80, 92, 94
Skidegate, 54
Smallpox, viii. *See also* Tsimshian: and smallpox
'Small shoes for feet too large,' 81
Smithe, William (Chief Commissioner of Lands and Works), 76, 78-9
Spanish model of conquest, viii; French imitation of, viii
Sproat, Gilbert M. (Indian Reserve Commissioner, 1876-80), 74
Sunday school, 41, 45
Superintendent-General of Indian Affairs. *See* Canada, government of: Department of Indian Affairs; Dewdney, Edgar; Macdonald, John A.; Mills, David
Sutherland, Alexander, 51, 58-9, 71-2, 85, 92
Swanson, David 71

Tate, Charles M., 41, 44, 62
Tate, Henry, 53, 118 n.2
Tate, Robert, 53
Taylor, William 'California,' 27, 28, 33
Temlaham. See Downfall of Temlaham
Temperance Society, 70
Tlingit, 15-6
Todd, Charles (Indian Agent), 82-3, 86, 88-90
Tomlinson, Rev. Robert, 54

Tsimshian: aims in sending for missionary, x-xi, 25, 39-40, 42, 55, 61, 108-22; analysis of response to missions, 96-105, 107-11; and Band of Christian Workers, 55, 88, 91-3, 111; and competition between Anglicans and Methodists, 39-43; and control of mission, x-xi, 59, 61, 72, 87-91, 93, 109, 111 (*see also* Tsimshian: Band of Christian Workers); and conversion process, 108-9, 111 (*see also* Conversion; Culture); and Crosby, initial acceptance, 61; culture, analytic problems, 3-5 (*see also* Culture); and Duncan, response to, 22-5; and economic change, 49, 71-2, 88, 90-2 (*see also* Crosby: and secular life; Duncan: mission philosophy); and exogamy, 69-70; frustrations with Crosby, 50-6, 71-2, 92; and Indian Advancement Act, 78, 80-4, 86-7, 89-90; and land question, x, 44, 50, 72-88, 90, 93, 109 (*see also* British Columbia, government of; Canada, government of; Crosby; Methodist Church of Canada; Superintendent-General of Indian Affairs); linguistic divisions, 5; mobility, 6, 49, 72, 109; natural environment, 11-14, 18-20; persistence of traditions after conversion, 48, 68-71, 131 n.34, 138 n.26; potlatch, 6-11, 16-18, 21, 25, 35-6, 47, 50, 68-70, 85, 88, 119 n.26; religion (traditional), 8-14; and religious acculturation program, 44-8; response to Crosby's revivalism, 44-8 (*see also* Crosby: and revivalism); and secular acculturation program, 61-7 (*see also* Crosby: and secular life); self-government, 87-91; and smallpox, 16-17, 23, 47, 97, 120 n.4; social system, 5-7, 10-11, 14, 20; syncretism, 50, 126 n.21; trade with Europeans, 16-20 (*see also* Fur trade; Hudson's Bay Company); village council (Crosby creation), 52, 64, 67-8, 70, 81, 83, 89, 109; winter ceremonies, 6, 9, 12-13, 19-21, 39-40, 50-67, 107

Tsimshian Proper. *See* Tsimshian

Usher, Jean, 17, 22-4, 44, 96-7, 104-5

Vankoughnet, Lawrence (Deputy Superintendent-General of Indian Affairs), 78, 83, 85-7
Victoria, BC, 43, 53; Crosby's arrival in, 34; Kate Dudoward's conversion in, 39-40, 44, 51; and land question, 73, 76, 78-9, 85; as trade centre for Tsimshian after 1850, 17-18, 20-2, 25, 97
Victoria Daily Colonist, 75-6, 82

Victorian values, 20-1, 23-5, 35, 62, 65-6
Vowell, A.W. (Indian Superintendent), 86, 89-90

Wallace, Chief Herbert, 69, 85, 88, 90
War of 1812, 31
Warren, Max, 102
Wellington, Arthur (Clah), 76-7, 85
Wesley, John, 28-32
Wesleyan Methodist Church. *See* Methodist Church, Wesleyan
Western Methodist Recorder, 99
White, Rev. Edward, 28, 35
Williams, Henry, 101
Williscroft, Mr., 66
Withrow, W.H., 103
Woodstock, 26-7
Woodsworth, James, 91
Wooton, S.Y., 82
Work, John, 17, 76
Wright, Thomas, 51

Young, Rev. Egerton Ryerson, 36

Zaslow, Morris, 96, 104

Printed in Canada on acid-free paper ∞
Set in Palatino by The Typeworks, Vancouver, BC
Printed and bound in Canada by John Deyell Company
Lindsay, Ontario

Copy-editor: Joanne Richardson
Proofreader: Joy Tataryn
Jacket design: George Vaitkunas